INTERDISCIPLINARY INSTRUCTION

A Practical Guide for Elementary and Middle School Teachers

KARLYN E. WOOD
State University of New York
College at Old Westbury

Merrill,
an imprint of Prentice Hall
Upper Saddle River, New Jersey   Columbus, Ohio

Library of Congress Cataloging-in-Publication Data

Wood, Karlyn E.
    Interdisciplinary instruction : a practical guide for elementary and middle school teachers /
Karlyn E. Wood.
      p. cm.
    Includes bibliographical references and index.
    ISBN 0-13-227760-3
    1. Interdisciplinary approach in education—United States. 2. Education, Elementary—
United States—Curricula. 3. Middle schools—United States—Curricula. 4. Curriculum
planning—United States. I. Title.
  LB1570.W644 1997
  375′.001—dc20

96-8118
CIP

Cover art: Lauretta Tiell
Editor: Debbie Stollenwerk
Production Editor: Sheryl Glicker Langner
Design Coordinator: Jill E. Bonar
Text Designer: Anne Flanagan
Cover Designer: Anne Flanagan
Production Manager: Laura Messerly
Director of Marketing: Kevin Flanagan
Advertising/Marketing Coordinator: Julie Shough
Electronic Text Management: Marilyn Wilson Phelps, Matthew Williams, Karen L. Bretz, Tracey
    Ward

This book was set in Zapf International by Prentice Hall and was printed and bound by
R.R. Donnelley & Sons Company. The cover was printed by Phoenix Color Corp.

 © 1997 by Prentice-Hall, Inc.
Simon & Schuster/A Viacom Company
Upper Saddle River, New Jersey 07458

Photo credits: p. 1 by K.S. Studios/Merrill/Prentice Hall; pp. 11 and 51 by Anne Vega/Merrill/
Prentice Hall; pp. 19, 31, 81, and 115 by Scott Cunningham/Merrill/Prentice Hall.

Printed in the United States of America

10 9 8 7 6 5 4 3 2 1

ISBN: 0-13-227760-3

Prentice-Hall International (UK) Limited, *London*
Prentice-Hall of Australia Pty. Limited, *Sydney*
Prentice-Hall of Canada, Inc., *Toronto*
Prentice-Hall Hispanoamericana, S. A., *Mexico*
Prentice-Hall of India Private Limited, *New Delhi*
Prentice-Hall of Japan, Inc., *Tokyo*
Simon & Schuster Asia Pte. Ltd., *Singapore*
Editora Prentice-Hall do Brasil, Ltda., *Rio de Janeiro*

To Louise, Kim, Nina and Jennifer.

To my students and colleagues in the Teacher Education Program at the State University of New York/College at Old Westbury.

PREFACE

*T*raditionally, instruction in our schools has been organized in a manner that tends to treat the academic disciplines—or subject areas—separately from one another. In contrast, **interdisciplinary** instruction always begins with a central theme; students then investigate the theme using any disciplines that can assist in their inquiry. The interdisciplinary themes students study vary greatly. Some are typical of topics usually included in a social studies or science curriculum; however, themes from other disciplines, such as literature, mathematics, visual arts, and performing arts, can also be used for interdisciplinary studies.

Recently, there appears to be a renewed interest among educators in the interdisciplinary method. That interest has been stimulated by legislative steps that have been taken by some state departments of education. The New York State Education Department, for example, currently requires teachers in grades three through six to develop at least one interdisciplinary project with students in their classes each year. As a result of that kind of legislation, teachers and administrators are showing considerable interest in program designs for interdisciplinary instruction and in practical ways to plan for its use in the classroom. Many teachers are eager to learn exactly what interdisciplinary *projects* should involve and how to distinguish them from other instructional activities they currently use with students.

The interdisciplinary approach is usually more familiar to early childhood teachers than it is to those who teach in the intermediate grades or middle school. Preschool and kindergarten teachers routinely plan their instructional programs around central themes, themes which are then used as much as feasible in teaching daily lessons and activities. Most primary grade teachers feel that they understand the method and that they have been prepared for it in their college programs. At the intermediate and middle school levels, however, teachers may feel they have less experience with the interdisciplinary approach than their early childhood colleagues.

The purpose of this book is to provide preservice and inservice elementary and middle school teachers and administrators with a handbook that introduces the interdisciplinary method and offers practical suggestions about how to carry it out.

I have based the book partly on the materials I prepared for my classes. I have purposefully kept the theoretical chapters succinct so that the emphasis can be on the *thinking processes* involved in designing the two types of interdisciplinary unit plans: thematic and research-oriented thematic units. In order to give emphasis to the planning processes and to illustrate the essentials of those processes as clearly as possible, examples are given for each step in the unit planning processes outlined in Chapters 5 and 6. The models in this book illustrate *one* way to design interdisciplinary units but, of course, not the *only* way. The point of view expressed throughout this book is that no single planning format will work satisfactorily for every teacher.

This book is intended for use in methods courses at both the undergraduate and graduate levels, and it is also appropriate for inservice courses in schools and teacher centers. The practical explanations and examples provided in the book should prove especially helpful for teachers who have not previously studied interdisciplinary instruction and would like to learn a way to get started.

College instructors who emphasize a constructivist approach in teaching and who advocate interdisciplinary methods in social studies, science, and generic methods courses can use this book to help students understand both the theoretical and practical aspects of interdisciplinary instruction. Instructors of reading and mathematics methods courses will find it useful to help students note the relationships between those disciplines and comprehensive interdisciplinary studies.

Organization of the Book

The early chapters provide a theoretical framework for the method. The first chapter reviews the theory supporting interdisciplinary instruction, outlines distinguishing features of the method, and reviews a rationale for using it with students in elementary and middle schools. The second chapter explores the child developmental base for the method. It explains the relationship between children's growing and changing intellectual abilities during the different developmental periods and provides an overview of the designs for two types of interdisciplinary units.

The primary requirements of teachers who plan to use the interdisciplinary approach are discussed in Chapter 3. That chapter emphasizes the need for both general and child development knowledge, a compatible educational philosophy, and the serious matter of excellence in classroom management skills. Chapter 3 also includes a review of major planning concerns, emphasizing the need for skills in unit planning, the application of learning principles, and the recognition of students' individual working and learning styles. Chapter 3 ends with a discussion of team teaching and the use of technology with the interdisciplinary approach.

The practical section begins in the fourth chapter of the book with a review of preliminary steps in the process of planning interdisciplinary units of study. Those preparatory steps include selecting unit themes and designing an interdisciplinary unit plan. General instructional strategies are also reviewed in the fourth chapter. Preparing instructional objectives, developing questioning techniques, determining levels of instruction, evaluating students' unit work, and establishing learning centers are included in the discussion.

Chapters 5 and 6 are specifically designed to teach the *processes* involved in thematic planning. Each chapter presents a suggested procedure along with a sequence of steps and examples to follow in designing a type of interdisciplinary unit plan. These planning chapters can be used by students during practicums in class. As they follow the steps to plan their own units, instructors will be able to use valuable class time to interact directly with students and critique the plans as they develop.

Chapter 5 details the processes involved in planning thematic units. Chapter 6 studies the research-oriented thematic unit, an alternate type of interdisciplinary unit plan for students at intermediate and middle school levels. Each chapter includes a detailed unit plan outline, followed by the planning procedure with examples at each step. Chapter 6 also suggests a way to plan and organize a research-oriented unit for use in a departmentalized school. At the end of each planning chapter is a complete version of the unit plan designed in the step-by-step explanation.

The final chapter presents a brief discussion of the process of change involved when teachers move toward an interdisciplinary program. It suggests ways school systems can help to support teachers as they work through that process. The chapter then concludes with a summary of major points introduced in the book. The appendix includes additional unit plan designs (webs), some of which were prepared by undergraduate teacher education majors.

In addition to chapter references, all chapters also include a list of suggested readings. The readings include early, theoretical works for students who would like additional background material or who plan to undertake their own research on topics included in the chapters. The lists also include writings that reflect current thinking and trends on those topics.

Acknowledgments

Our quest for knowledge is a lifelong pursuit in which we learn both from our experiences and from one another. Teachers often play an important role in facilitating this process. For most of us, some teachers will be especially well remembered for their positive contributions. I wish to thank two of my teachers. To begin, I consider myself fortunate to have been taught by Myrtle Cope, an exemplary master teacher. I want to thank her for the early influence she had on my decision to become an elementary teacher and for her constructivist approach which continues to influence my teaching practice.

I would also like to acknowledge the late Roland Chatterton, a forward-thinking educator and pioneer in multidisciplinary education. Dr. Chatterton introduced me to interdisciplinary methodology; it was his patient mentoring and guidance that facilitated my own development as an interdisciplinary teacher.

I would like to thank my wife, Louise, for her patience and support as I prepared the manuscript. My colleagues Jossie O'Neill and Gareth B. Wilmott provided me with their valuable feedback on drafts of the manuscript, and I want to thank them for their time and many helpful suggestions as the project developed.

I want to express my appreciation to the students who, while still in the process of learning about interdisciplinary planning, volunteered their unit plan designs for the appendix of the book. My colleagues in the Teacher Education Program at the State University of New York/College at Old Westbury have provided me with their support, and I thank them for their interest and encouragement throughout the project.

I particularly wish to thank my reviewers for their input and suggestions: JoAnne Buggey, University of Minnesota; Barbara Kacer, Western Kentucky University; Cynthia G. Kruger, University of Massachusetts, Dartmouth; Cynthia E. Ledbetter, University of Texas at Dallas; Linda S. Levstick, University of Kentucky; and Donna Merkley, Iowa State University.

I would like to acknowledge artist Nina Vassallo for the drawings she prepared for me that inspired and were adapted for the final design on the cover of this book.

Finally, I would like to acknowledge my editors at Merrill/Prentice Hall: Debbie Stollenwerk for her continuous interest, her counsel, guidance, and many professional suggestions as I prepared the manuscript; Rebecca Bobb for her expertise and the recommendations she made throughout the copy editing process; and Sheryl Langner for her guidance and support in the final production stages of the book.

TO THE READER

*W*hen I started teaching, I had little understanding of the interdisciplinary method, and I was certainly unaware of all I would have to learn over the next few years in order to use it in my own classroom. As a young, inexperienced teacher, I began my career in an elementary school district that was proud of its multidisciplinary philosophy. Teachers were expected to use a multidisciplinary approach at every level from kindergarten through the sixth grade. I began studying the method from the outset, but it was not until I observed the enthusiasm of the other teachers who had been using it for some time that I became committed to developing the skills I would need to carry it out myself.

Throughout the first two years, I found multidisciplinary—or interdisciplinary—teaching far more challenging than I had ever anticipated, and it is likely that had I not been given a great deal of moral support from other teachers and administrators in my school, I would have given the method up altogether. I learned from my colleagues how important it is to reserve extra time to plan for this kind of instruction and soon found myself spending countless hours after school trying to write plans for the interdisciplinary units I was teaching.

In those early experimental years, I paid little attention to planning *processes* and instead, spent most of my energy searching for the best way to write a unit plan. I realized that I needed to learn more about the planning process itself. In time, my concentration shifted from the *written* plan to the *thinking* involved in designing an interdisciplinary unit. I had discovered that the planning process was far more important than the format of the written plan. However, most of the attempts I made to locate information on the interdisciplinary approach or the unit planning process revealed that little substantive material appeared to be available.

Seventeen years later, when I began teaching education majors in college, I found that there was still a dearth of practical material written about interdisciplinary unit planning to use with my students. Out of necessity, I began preparing my own. To develop those materials, I drew upon my classroom teaching experience with the method and focused on the sequential thought processes involved in unit preparation.

Now, after using those materials for several years, I have found them to be especially helpful for students who are just beginning to learn about interdisciplinary instruction and unit planning. I have noted that when the materials are used in class, I need to spend less class time explaining the planning processes and giving repetitious verbal instructions about them. Instead, I have more time to work directly with students as they practice designing their own interdisciplinary unit plans.

It is my hope that this book will help both preservice and inservice teachers explore interdisciplinary instruction and the planning processes involved in it. I also hope that instructors will save valuable time by using this book and can use that time to help their students become better teachers.

CONTENTS

1
Interdisciplinary Instructional Theory and Rationale   *1*

Distinguishing Features of Interdisciplinary Instruction   2

    The Central Theme   2

    Use of Disciplines   3

    Emphasis on Process and Content   3

Rationale for Interdisciplinary Instruction in the Elementary and Middle School   4

    Development of Multiple Intelligences   4

    Social Interaction   5

    Meaningful Use of Academic Skills   6

    Benefits for Children with Special Needs   7

    Multiple Sources of Information   8

2
Child Development and Interdisciplinary Instruction   *11*

Development in Early Childhood Related to the Design of Thematic Units   12

    Involving Children in Planning Thematic Units   13

    Encouraging Children to Develop a Variety of Abilities   13

Development in Middle Childhood and Early Adolescence Related to the Design of Thematic and Research-Oriented Thematic Units   14

    Research-Oriented Thematic Units   15

3

Teaching Requirements and Concerns   19

Requirements   20

   General and Child Development Knowledge   20

   A Compatible Educational Philosophy   21

   Classroom Management Skills   21

Instructional Concerns   24

   Unit Planning   24

   Principles of Learning   24

   Individual Learning Styles   25

   Team Teaching and Interdisciplinary Instruction   25

   Technology   27

4

Preliminary Steps in the Unit Planning Process   31

Selecting Interdisciplinary Themes   32

Interdisciplinary Unit Plan Design   33

General Planning Strategies   34

   Preparing Instructional Objectives   34

   Determining Cognitive Levels of Instruction Using Bloom's Taxonomy   36

   Questioning   37

   Evaluating Children's Unit Work   38

   Planning Learning Centers   45

5

Designing Thematic Units   51

Thematic Unit Plan Outline   52

An Eight-Step Procedure for Developing a Thematic Unit Plan   54

   Step One: Considering Children's Developmental
Abilities and Background for the Theme   56

   Step Two: Brainstorming for Possible Procedures and
Preparing a Graphic Design or Web of the Procedures   58

   Step Three: Planning the Initial Lesson for the Unit   62

   Step Four: Describing Other Lessons and Activities   65

Step Five: Listing the General Unit Objectives   67

Step Six: Listing Tentative Evaluation Methods and Techniques   68

Step Seven: Listing Essential Materials   69

Step Eight: Deciding the Unit Title or Designing a
Method of Involving the Children in Creating a Title   69

"Spring"—A Sample Thematic Unit Plan   70

6

Designing Research-Oriented Thematic Units for Intermediate and Middle School Grades   81

Research-Oriented Thematic Unit Plan Outline   83

An Eight-Step Procedure for Developing
Research-Oriented Thematic Unit Plans   86

Step One: Considering the Students'
Developmental Abilities and Background   88

Step Two: Brainstorming to Develop Four Lists,
and Preparing the Graphic Design for the Unit   89

Step Three: Planning the Introductory Lesson   92

Step Four: Describing the Remainder of the Planning
Phase, and the Research and Reporting Phases   95

Step Five: Listing the General Unit Objectives   95

Step Six: Listing Tentative Evaluation Methods and Techniques   96

Step Seven: Listing Essential Materials   97

Step Eight: Deciding the Unit Title, or Developing a
Method for Involving Students in Creating a Title   97

"Deserts of the United States"—A Sample
Research-Oriented Thematic Unit Plan   97

Modifying a Research-Oriented Unit
Plan for a Departmentalized School   111

7

Interdisciplinary Instruction and the Change Process   115

Moving Toward an Interdisciplinary Program   116

Why Teachers Are Slow to Change Methods   116

Research and the Interdisciplinary Method   117

The Need for System Support   118
   Effecting Curricular Change   118
   Teacher and Classroom Needs   119
Conclusion   120
   Points in Support of Interdisciplinary Instruction   120
   Skills Required of Teachers   121
   Benefits to Children   121

Appendix   **123**
Index   **139**

1

Interdisciplinary Instructional Theory and Rationale

In the first chapter, the theoretical foundations of interdisciplinary instruction are reviewed. This discussion focuses on:

- *Several distinguishing features of interdisciplinary instruction.*
- *A rationale for using the interdisciplinary approach at the elementary and middle school levels.*

··

Distinguishing Features of Interdisciplinary Instruction

As elementary and middle school teachers instruct students in their classes, they often use a wide variety of methods and techniques, each of which has its own unique characteristics. Interdisciplinary instruction is an instructional approach that is also distinguished from other teaching methods by its special features.

A fundamental feature of the interdisciplinary approach is that students become involved in comprehensive instructional units of study. Interdisciplinary units have at least three unique characteristics:

1. Each interdisciplinary unit focuses on a central theme.
2. Students explore the central theme by using skills and techniques from a variety of disciplines.
3. The interdisciplinary method places equal emphasis on process and content.

The Central Theme

Instead of being subject or discipline centered, each interdisciplinary unit focuses on a central theme. The theme is explored by employing any disciplines—subjects or domains—that can help to inform the learner about the theme. In the primary grades, for example, themes such as "Our Family" or "Our Neighborhood" are typically studied because they are often recommended in state syllabi for the social studies curriculum. Other, less traditional themes, however, can often afford more opportunities for young children to apply their inquiry skills and creativity. For example, themes such as "Changes," "Environments," "Flying," and "How It Works" can offer interesting, challenging inquiries that are feasible for early interdisciplinary studies.

Older students can usually investigate more sophisticated, comprehensive themes with titles like "Mediterranean Lands," "The Middle East," "Westward Expansion," and "Our Endangered Environment." Although many themes such as these are traditional for older students, interdisciplinary themes can develop from any discipline, subject, or domain, including the sciences, children's literature, mathematics, music, and the arts.

An interesting and exceptionally well developed example of an interdisciplinary unit that begins with the arts and evolves to include all areas of the curriculum is "Spaces and Places," a thematic unit designed by Pappas, Kiefer, and Levstik (1995) for students in an upper elementary grade. Elwyn Richardson (1964), an elementary teacher in New Zealand, also used the arts as the basis for his unusual interdisciplinary program. After completing art projects using raw materials from their rural environment, Richardson involved the children in his school in extensive related activities in writing, reading, science, and mathematics.

Use of Disciplines

While students are involved in studying holistic, interdisciplinary themes, they are also being exposed to the skills and ways of knowing inherent in the different disciplines they use to investigate those themes. They are encouraged to think critically about the issues inherent in their studies and to use the skills and techniques from any disciplines that can assist them in their investigation.

In thematic studies, students have many natural opportunities to observe the connections and to note relationships among the various disciplines they employ in their study. Jacobs (1989) emphasizes this characteristic when she suggests that in interdisciplinary units, the teacher intentionally "applies methodology and language from more than one discipline to examine a central theme, issue, problem, topic, or experience" (p. 8).

Emphasis on Process and Content

Another distinguishing feature of the interdisciplinary method is that, whereas disciplinary, subject-centered instruction focuses almost exclusively on content and aims largely at helping children amass facts and general information, interdisciplinary instruction is equally concerned with the learning *processes, skills, and ways of knowing* that are unique to the different disciplines, subjects, or domains. Although there is no consensus about which of the processes are most important, those involved in inquiry and scientific investigation are especially useful in interdisciplinary studies. There has also been an ongoing debate among educators for years about the importance of *process* versus *content*; however, that particular debate is of little concern to interdisciplinary teachers because they tend to agree with Dewey's (1916) advice that equal importance be attributed to content and process. They expect their students to amass facts and develop concepts while they practice important academic learning processes that will "become the models [they will use] for later exploratory behaviors." (Gardner, 1993a, p. 31) and gain insights about and practice different ways of knowing. At intermediate and middle school grade levels, students undertake more complex forms of inquiry, making use of processes that naturally stimulate the higher level thinking and reasoning skills.

Finally, although gaining knowledge and practicing the learning processes are major aims in interdisciplinary instruction, students also have many meaningful opportunities to practice their reading, writing, and computational skills while they are involved in authentic investigations.

Rationale for Interdisciplinary Instruction in the Elementary and Middle School

Why should interdisciplinary instruction be used at the elementary and middle school levels? Before answering this question, consider how a group of children are likely to receive instruction about a specific social studies theme in a school with a traditional approach to curriculum. Observe how one group was taught about the island nation of Japan over an eight-year period:

> In the first grade, where children often study concepts of the family, their teacher read them stories about families from several cultures around the world; one story was about a Japanese family. A music teacher taught the children a Japanese folk song in the second grade and a traditional Japanese dance in the third grade. In the fourth grade, an art teacher helped the children experiment with origami. The children also studied geographical regions of the world in their fourth grade year; there was some discussion of islands and island nations in that study. Finally, in middle school, the children studied aspects of Asian cultures, including Japanese culture.

The sequence in the above description is characteristic of a traditional, subject-centered approach to a social topic. Instead of an integrated inquiry of Japan and Japanese culture at any specific grade level, the children were offered isolated bits of information in a fragmented study that was spread out over an eight-year period.

At first, it may seem logical to approach a social study this way; certainly, we know that adults are capable of integrating related information they receive about any topic over a long period of time. However, we also know that it may be more difficult for very young children to do so. Gardner (1991) suggests that the mind of a young child—five to seven or even ten years of age—is intuitive, resourceful, highly imaginative and creative, but at the same time, it is limited by a "tendency to stereotype and simplify" (pp. 110–111). "It contains a swirl of symbols, scripts, theories, and incipient notions and concepts, which can be involved in appropriate ways but which also remain to be sorted out in a more secure manner" (p. 111). Earlier, Piaget and Inhelder (1975) found that the thinking of young children tends to be *centered;* in their minds, isolated concepts and bits of information tend to remain unrelated. In view of these limitations, an important reason for using an integrated or interdisciplinary method is that by approaching studies thematically and holistically, students may be able to overcome a tendency to misinterpret and instead make better sense of their world.

Development of Multiple Intelligences

An especially strong argument for an interdisciplinary approach evolves from Gardner's (1983, 1993b) theory of **multiple intelligences.** This theory strongly suggests that human beings operate in at least seven—possibly more—intelligence areas:

- **linguistic or verbal intelligence** (the ability to use language well and to learn through verbal methods such as reading, note taking, writing summaries and reports, and conducting interviews)
- **logical-mathematical intelligence** (using mathematics and logic, forming hypotheses, and conducting scientific inquiries)
- **spatial intelligence** (detecting spatial relationships, noticing likenesses and differences visually, creating art and design, and thinking by visualizing in pictures)
- **musical intelligence** (using music as a tool for thinking, demonstrating feelings and attitudes with music, and associating thought with music)
- **bodily-kinesthetic intelligence** (using the entire body to help master or to explain ideas and concepts)
- **interpersonal intelligence** (understanding others, working effectively and cooperatively with other people, and sharing tasks and responsibilities)
- **intrapersonal intelligence** (understanding oneself and being able to analyze one's own performance in order to grow and change)

Gardner suggests that his "theory gives educators a way of thinking about individual gifts and how to accommodate teaching to them" (Brandt, 1988, p. 34). Thus, if students are developing in any or all of these intelligence areas, it is logical to conclude that they need opportunities to grow in more than one at a time. It would logically follow that interdisciplinary studies in the elementary school should replace isolated, subject-centered, disciplinary instruction. Doing so would thus facilitate optimal development for more students, mainly because the interdisciplinary method naturally provides for individual development in the different intelligence areas Gardner proposes.

Gardner's theory is as important for the middle school as it is for the earlier grades. His theory not only lends support for the interdisciplinary approach, but is also consistent with one of the eight recommendations from the 1989 Carnegie Council's Task Force on Education of Young Adolescents to "teach a core academic program" ("The Seventh Grade Slump," 1992, p. 3). The core curriculum is an interdisciplinary concept which Reed and Bergmann (1995) describe as " . . . the integration of a variety of disciplines around a single core, often a theme or a problem" (p. 313). Clearly, this notion is consistent with the idea that students should have opportunities for development in more than one domain or intelligence area, again suggestive of the interdisciplinary method.

Social Interaction

Students also need opportunities for the kind of social interaction and guidance teachers and capable peers can provide quite naturally in the course of interdisciplinary studies. Piaget (1964) believed that verbal interaction between students and teachers was indeed necessary to develop arbitrary social concepts; however, he did not believe that the use of direct instruction was as important in developing physical and logico-mathematical knowledge. Further, he cautioned against too much use of verbal instruction or demonstrations, especially with very young children, because those methods might actually inhibit the development of operational (generalizable, useful) knowledge.

Today, however, there is considerable evidence suggesting that Piaget may have attributed too little importance to instruction in the development of concepts. For example, the importance of social interaction and culture in promoting optimal learning is clear in Vygotsky's theory that there is a ***zone of proximal development*** or ***ZPD*** (Vygotsky, 1978, 1986). The ZPD is "the distance between the actual developmental level as determined by independent problem solving and the level of potential development as determined through problem solving under adult guidance or in collaboration with more capable peers" (Vygotsky, 1978, p. 86).

Contemporary researchers agree with Vygotsky on the importance of culture and social interaction in the process of knowledge acquisition. In Canada, for example, studies of early development support Vygotsky's theory regarding the impact of social interaction and instruction in early childhood on cognitive development as children mature (Case, 1985). Case also suggests the importance of interdisciplinary instruction in promoting children's problem-solving skills "across as wide a range of culturally valued problem domains or subjects as possible" (p. 393).

Wertsch (1985) offers a particularly comprehensive discussion of Vygotsky's theory on the value of social interaction, and in *Acts of Meaning*, Bruner (1990) talks of the importance of adult interaction and instruction in helping children make "narrative" sense of actions and ideas. Forman, Minick, and Stone (1993) also provide a compelling argument for interdisciplinary studies—what the authors refer to as *theme research projects*—in their review of Vygotsky's theory and its implications for classroom practice. Interdisciplinary, thematic studies provide natural opportunities for the kind of instruction and teacher/student, student/student interaction these contemporary researchers find critical for optimal learning.

Meaningful Use of Academic Skills

Another reason to use interdisciplinary instruction in the elementary grades and middle school is simply that most real problems in life are investigated and/or solved by using more than one discipline at a time. For example, when purchasing a new home, economics is obviously a major factor but not the only one. Location (geography), architectural style, educational facilities, and other community resources also need to be considered before a final decision can be made. Interdisciplinary instruction routinely and realistically encourages children to use the skills and ways of knowing associated with any disciplines that can be applied logically in their investigations.

Every teacher is concerned about students' academic skills and with providing sufficient practice in those skills. The exercises children continue to be given in many schools in workbooks and on dittos have little or no relationship to the themes they are studying. Those exercises then simply become practice *for the sake of practice*.

In contrast to this type of skills practice, "almost any subject . . . is best taught when it is needed to accomplish something else" (Wakefield, 1993, p. 137). Interdisciplinary instruction is in step with this idea because it always provides for the application of skills in meaningful contexts. As unit themes are explored, students find that they *need* to use their inquiry skills, *need* to read for information, *need* to write letters and reports and to give oral presentations in front of the class. Students employ mathematical skills as they prepare charts, graphs, and maps; they follow the scientific method as they work with related science experiments and activities; they also explore drama, music, and dance and gain experience with various art media. In fact, the interdisciplinary approach can provide so many spontaneous, purposeful opportunities for students to practice their skills, prepare projects, and work with construction materials that teachers who have previously used artificial dittos and other conventional practice materials, which isolate skills from a meaningful context, may no longer feel the need to use those materials.

Benefits for Children with Special Needs

Today, another important motivation for using the interdisciplinary method is its effectiveness as an appropriate alternative to traditional approaches for children with special needs. In 1975, Public Law 94–142, The Education of All Handicapped Children Act, was enacted, mandating that children with handicapping conditions be placed in the least restrictive instructional environment possible, preferably in regular classrooms. In order to comply with this regulation, classroom teachers had to begin working with children who had previously been taught separately in special classes. Most "regular" classroom teachers had little or no specific preparation for their new role, so they have needed to experiment on their own and try creative approaches and methods in order to include—not just accommodate—their new students.

Many children still need to spend part of the school day in special assistance settings outside their regular classrooms. Their frequent absence from the classroom can make it difficult for teachers to include them in the regular program of activities. The flexibility afforded by the interdisciplinary method can help teachers, at least in part, to overcome this problem. This is possible because interdisciplinary units are usually completed over a period of time, and it is not necessary for all children in the class to be present at the same time in order to participate. Those who leave the room for special help can work on unit assignments when they return or at other times during the day.

Also, because children are encouraged to use a wide variety of resources to locate information, those who have difficulty reading for information can use alternative methods, such as interviewing, studying pictures, viewing films or filmstrips, and interacting with computer software programs. These and other materials can be selected carefully to ensure that they involve little or no reading. Reports need not be limited to writing papers or answering questions from a textbook selection; students can use alternatives, such as performing demonstrations, painting pictures and murals, and preparing dioramas and other constructions to show the concepts they have gained.

Multiple Sources of Information

A final point in support of the interdisciplinary approach is that because children use materials from many sources when they are engaged in research, it is easier to ensure that they are presented with a more inclusive view of history and historical events than is feasible when they need to rely on only one or two textbooks. In contrast to conventional approaches, no single textbook is used exclusively in an interdisciplinary program. Instead, classrooms are equipped with textbooks in social studies, science, language arts, and other disciplines from many different publishers; in each classroom, the available materials are written at, below, and above grade level to accommodate as many ability levels as possible. Trade books and literature related to the unit theme are borrowed from public and school libraries. Teachers ensure that a wide variety of materials is available to provide children with greater access to information about the contributions of all ethnic and racial groups. They can ascertain if children's resource materials adequately address human rights issues, such as slavery, the holocaust, genocide, and other world problems which are sometimes given minimal treatment or neglected altogether in a single textbook.

The significance of this kind of exposure for students today is effectively dramatized in a statement by Milagros Henriquez, a recent graduate in teacher education, as she accepted an award for outstanding work related to multicultural education: "Multicultural education is *basic* education for students in the twenty-first century" (Henriquez, 1995). In our multicultural society, students need access to information that only a rich variety of materials can provide.

References

Brandt, R. (1988). On assessment in the arts: A conversation with Howard Gardner. *Educational Leadership, 45*(4), 30–34.

Bruner, J. (1990). *Acts of meaning.* Cambridge, MA: Harvard University Press.

Case, R. (1985). *Intellectual development: Birth to adulthood.* Orlando, FL: Academic Press.

Dewey, J. (1916). *Democracy and education.* New York: The Free Press.

Forman, E. A., Minick, N., & Stone, C. A. (1993). *Contexts for learning.* New York: Oxford University Press.

Gardner, H. (1983). *Frames of mind: The theory of multiple intelligences.* New York: Basic Books.

Gardner, H. (1991). *The unschooled mind: How children think and how schools should teach.* New York: Basic Books.

Gardner, H. (1993a). *Creating minds.* New York: Basic Books.

Gardner, H. (1993b). *Multiple intelligences: The theory in practice.* New York: Basic Books.

Henriquez, M. (Speaker). (1995). Acceptance speech at the academic awards ceremony of the Teacher Education Program at the State University of New York/College at Old Westbury.

Jacobs, H. (Ed.). (1989). *Interdisciplinary curriculum: Design and implementation.* Alexandria, VA: Association for Supervision and Curriculum Development.

Pappas, C. C., Kiefer, B. Z., & Levstik, L. S. (1995). *An integrated language perspective in the elementary school.* White Plains, NY: Longman.

Piaget, J. (1970). *Science of education and the psychology of the child.* New York: Orion.

Piaget, J., & Inhelder, B. (1975). *The origin of the idea of chance in children.* New York: W. W. Norton.

Reed, J. S., & Bergmann, V. E. (1995). *In the classroom: An introduction to education* (2nd ed.). Guilford, CT: Dushkin.

Richardson, E. S. (1964). *In the early world.* New York: Pantheon Books.

The seventh grade slump and how to avoid it. (1992, January/February). *The Harvard Education Letter, 8*(1), 1–4.

Vygotsky, L. S. (1978). *Mind in society: The development of higher psychological processes.* Cambridge, MA: Harvard University Press.

Vygotsky, L. S. (1986). *Thought and language.* Cambridge, MA: MIT Press.

Wakefield, A. P. (1993). Developmentally appropriate practice: "Figuring things out." *The Educational Forum, 57*(2), 134–43.

Wertsch, J. V. (1985). *Vygotsky and the social formation of the mind.* Cambridge, MA: Harvard University Press.

Suggested Readings

The following readings are included to supplement the references in this chapter. The list includes both historical and contemporary materials that provide additional background information on interdisciplinary methodology and its rationale; some readings address the need for change and offer suggestions for the change process.

Bruner, J. (1960). *The process of education.* New York: Vintage Books.

Charbonneau, M. P., & Reider, B. E. (1995). *The integrated elementary classroom: A developmental model of education for the 21st century.* Needham Heights, MA: Allyn & Bacon.

Clark, B. (1986). *Optimizing learning: The integrative education model in the classroom.* Upper Saddle River, NJ: Merrill/Prentice Hall.

Cole, H. P. (1972). *Process education: The new direction for elementary-secondary schools.* Upper Saddle River, NJ: Educational Technology Publications.

Dewey, J. (1933). *How we think.* Boston: D. C. Heath.

Dewey, J. (1938). *Experience and education.* London: Collier-Macmillan.

Frymier, J. R. (1973). *A school for tomorrow.* Berkeley, CA: McCutchan.

Jacob, S. H. (1982a). Piaget and education: Aspects of a theory. *The Educational Forum, 46*(2), 265–82.

Jacob, S. H. (1982b). Piaget and education: Aspects of a theory. *The Educational Forum, 46*(3), 221–38.

Jenkins, J. M. (1994). *World class schools: An evolving concept.* Reston, VA: National Association of Secondary School Principals.

Katz, L., & Chard, S. C. (1989). *Engaging children's minds: The project approach.* Norwood, NJ: Ablex Publishing.

Mason, E. (1972). *Collaborative learning.* New York: Agathon Press.

Ramsden, P. (Ed.). (1988). *Improving learning.* London: Kogan Page.

Silberman, C. E. (1970). *Crisis in the classroom: The remaking of American education.* New York: Random House.

Stevenson, C., & Carr, J. F. (Eds.). (1993). *Integrated studies in the middle grades.* New York: Teachers College Press.

White, A. M. (Ed.). (1981). *Interdisciplinary teaching.* San Francisco: Jossey–Bass.

2

Child Development and Interdisciplinary Instruction

This chapter explains how children's intellectual characteristics at different age levels influence the structure and design of interdisciplinary units. The chapter discusses:

- *Development in early childhood related to the design of an early childhood thematic unit.*
- *Development in middle childhood and early adolescence related to the design of thematic instruction and the research-oriented thematic unit— an alternative design for the intermediate grades and middle school.*

*T*hematic units of study can be used at all levels of the elementary and middle school, and as students mature, their changing developmental abilities allow them to undertake studies that are more and more sophisticated. Another type of thematic unit, that involves a more advanced research procedure—the research-oriented thematic unit—can be used by teachers as an alternative way to approach thematic studies. That type of thematic unit is an appropriate alternative for students in the intermediate elementary grades and middle school who have become more experienced and proficient in their research skills and who are also capable of reading for information independently.

Development in Early Childhood Related to the Design of Thematic Units

Piaget often stressed the importance of recognizing that, at all age levels, children's thinking characteristics have a significant effect on the kinds of academic work they are able to undertake (1976, 1974, 1973, 1970, 1966, 1955). Piaget's research also led him to conclude that the thinking and reasoning of children in the primary grades were dominated by **preoperational thought** (Phillips, 1981; Piaget & Inhelder, 1969). For many years, Piaget's unchallenged research led us to believe that all young children were highly egocentric and that their thinking was extremely centered during the early childhood years.

Since Piaget completed his work, contemporary researchers—often referred to as neo-Piagetian and post-Piagetian researchers—have found that Piaget had underestimated the abilities of children in the preschool and early elementary years (Flavell, 1985). These researchers have found young children to be less egocentric than Piaget had believed. Also, Piaget never considered the impact of social interaction as seriously as both Vygotsky (1986) and the post-Piagetians. Several post-Piagetians have already been cited in support of interdisciplinary instruction (Gardner, 1991, 1993; Forman, Minick, & Stone, 1993; Bruner, 1990; Case, 1985; Wertsch, 1985).

Although Piaget's work can still provide us with important information about children's intellectual development, it is clear that, contrary to Piaget's belief, intellectual development appears to proceed in a continuous manner and there is considerable influence both from our culture and from instruction on children's cognitive development. Santrock (1995) affirms this notion with: "Most contemporary developmentalists agree that children's cognitive development is not as grand stagelike as Piaget thought" (p. 387). Information is *processed*, and learners improve steadily in their ability to absorb and store knowledge from their environment (Berk, 1996).

Involving Children in Planning Thematic Units

Although the teacher will take the major responsibility for planning a thematic unit in the early grades, it is important to provide opportunities for young children to participate as much as they are able in the design of their study, and to incorporate their suggestions and special interests as a thematic unit develops. Once a theme has been selected, the teacher guides the planning process with the children so that several disciplines are integrated in the study. Children are then helped to note relationships of the various disciplines to the central theme of their unit. Although the teacher's long-term goal will be to help the children become independent in the planning process of their own studies, it is wise to proceed slowly until the children have developed adequate skill in doing so. Gardner (1995, January 6) emphasizes this idea:

> The educator of the future needs to walk a fine line—always encouraging the youngster to stretch, praising her when she succeeds, but equally important, providing support and a non-condemnatory interpretative framework when things do not go well. Eventually, aspiring creators can supply much of this support, scaffolding and interpreting framework for themselves. (p. 15)

In early childhood, children's perceptions may be influenced by some of the traditional Piagetian characteristics, such as having difficulty reversing thought patterns and following transformations. Their sense of time, history, and relationships develops slowly, and it is possible that some lingering egocentricity will interfere with their participation in cooperative group activities (Wadsworth, 1996; Flavell, 1985; Furth, 1971).

Encouraging Children to Develop a Variety of Abilities

Of course, all children are unique in their mental makeup, learning styles, and abilities. Gardner's proposition that "people have different cognitive strengths and contrasting cognitive styles" suggests that children should have opportunities to develop simultaneously in more than one cognitive area (1993, p. 6). If, therefore, teachers consider children's *multiple intelligences*, young children should be encouraged to undertake inquiries and to use reporting methods that are not always exclusively dependent on their linguistic ability. Using music, art media, and movement to investigate and to demonstrate mastery of concepts can supplement or even replace traditional book learning at times.

For many young children, inquiries that rely exclusively on reading can be difficult, mainly because there are relatively few resources on some themes for them to read independently. Instead, early childhood classrooms should offer an environment that has a rich and abundant supply of materials and learning activities, one that allows them to become *active participants* in their own learning (NCSS Task Force, 1989). When developing concepts, activities involving "hands-on" learning will be more helpful to young children than are abstract materials which generally rely on linguistic and mathematical abilities. Providing concrete opportunities will be especially important for the inclusion of children with special needs.

Those who have specific talents—artistic, musical, physical, linguistic, mathematical, etc.—should be challenged to undertake forms of inquiry that make use of their special abilities. Children who are capable of reading for information and preparing written reports should be encouraged to do so.

As a thematic unit reaches its conclusion, some culminating activity should be planned to help the children summarize the major concepts they have gained from their study.

Development in Middle Childhood and Early Adolescence Related to the Design of Thematic and Research-Oriented Thematic Units

Thematic units for students in the intermediate grades and middle school follow the same basic structure as those designed for younger children. However, they differ in both the quantity and level of work that can be required; substantially more reading and reporting activities can be added. Most students at the intermediate and middle school levels will have already achieved what Piaget and Inhelder (1969) describe as **concrete operational thought,** a pattern of thinking and reasoning that allows students to deal with more abstract concepts and systems of concepts, provided they first have some personal or direct experience to which to relate those concepts. Piaget believed that some students approach **formal operational thought** in their early adolescent years, enabling them to engage in genuine hypothetical thinking. However, Piaget gave less attention to the importance of individual differences, culture, and instruction on cognitive development; like the challenges to Piaget's early childhood theory, estimates of development in middle childhood and the early adolescent period are undergoing revision by post-Piagetianists. For example, it is likely that many young adolescents do not achieve the formal operational thinking patterns Piaget found from his studies (Santrock, 1996).

Ordinarily, older students can read better, and it is possible to find more suitable independent reading and other resource materials for them to use. Their improved skills also enable them to make increasing use of computer technology and, if available, local and distance networking, on-line, and Internet services. In the intermediate grades and middle school, students continue to need opportunities to acquire knowledge using their individual working and learning styles and multiple intelligences. In an interesting model program, called the *Key School*, teachers apply the principles of an "MI (multiple intelligences) curriculum." Students in the program participate on a regular basis in the activities of computing, music, and "bodily-kinesthetics," in addition to theme-centered curricula that embody the standard literacies and subject matter. . . . Each student participates each day in an apprenticeship-like "pod," where he works with peers of different ages and a competent teacher to master a craft or discipline of interest. (Gardner, 1993, p. 113)

Students in the Key School investigate several themes each year, including those with titles like "Patterns," "Connections," "The Renaissance—Then and Now," and "Mexican Heritage." These are interdisciplinary, thematic investigations.

Research-Oriented Thematic Units

Thematic studies of this type can be approached in the intermediate and middle school grades using a variation of the thematic unit planning structure used with younger children: the ***research-oriented thematic unit*** plan. This type of unit can usually be developed with children beginning in the second half of grade three. In middle and late childhood, most students are able to read independently for information, and they are becoming more proficient in the disciplines they have been meeting during their early years of school. Because they are able to cooperate better with one another, they enjoy cooperative group and committee work. Older students can also participate fully with the teacher in helping to design their units of study; they can plan their research by raising questions and suggesting problems to solve.

Planning and Organizing Research

The teacher plans and introduces a research-oriented thematic unit to the students. Then, while guiding them through the planning phase for their research, the teacher encourages students to participate in raising the questions to be answered and in suggesting general areas to be investigated.

Socially, older children usually enjoy working on ***committees*** where they share tasks and become involved in making group decisions. (A committee is a small cooperative learning group established to investigate and report on a specific subtopic or section of a research-oriented thematic unit. More specific information on using committees with research-oriented thematic units can be found in Chapter 6.)

Under teacher direction, the students next become involved in organizing their research theme into manageable component subtopics. To complete the planning phase of the unit, a research committee is formed to investigate each of the subtopics. Finally, each committee outlines specifically what the group needs to research, and each student assumes responsibility for a specific aspect of the committee's work.

The care needed when organizing any type of cooperative group work applies to a research committee. Readers are referred to the extensive discussions on cooperative learning found in a number of other publications (Arends, 1995; Slavin, 1995; Kauchak & Eggen, 1989; Slavin, Sharan, Kagan, Hertz-Lazarowitz, Webb, & Schmuck, 1985). In those and other sources, numerous practical suggestions are offered about the design and structure of cooperative learning activities. Also of interest is Dembo's (1988) comprehensive summary of findings from research on the use of cooperative learning in the classroom.

Completing Committee Reports

Committee work continues until each member has contributed his or her findings to the small group and the committee members have decided how they will report to the whole class. When committees begin to complete their work, the teacher schedules group presentations for them to report their findings to the class as a whole. To help maintain interest and to avoid monotony, committee reporting needs to vary in form. Students can be encouraged to use alternatives to conventional, individual oral reports; panel discussions, music and dance presentations, puppet shows, skits, experiments, demonstrations and displays of artifacts, maps, constructions, and art projects are some possible reporting forms. As each committee reports its findings, other students in the class are encouraged to take notes about what they learn from the report. After the completion of a committee report, the teacher helps the class to develop an outline of the most important information the committee has contributed during its presentation.

Throughout the unit, the teacher is responsible for outlining tasks clearly, providing opportunities for students with different styles of learning to gain the information they are seeking, ensuring that the research process guides children's work and, in general, encouraging responsible, productive work from everyone. The teacher may arrange field trips and on-line conferences using computer networking services. Films, filmstrips, and video presentations may be shown at logical points during the development of the unit. Relevant computer software programs, CD-ROM titles, and other suitable media material can be suggested for students to use for their research. Lessons are always needed in the important locational and notetaking skills.

Teachers often require some form of report from both individual students and committees. Reporting techniques can respect individual learning preferences; for example, one student may present an art project, another some movement or dance presentation, others may complete written reports or be part of a panel discussion. Of course, clear instructions need to be given about forms to be followed for any written or oral reports. In the intermediate grades, a committee report may be a simple compiling of the written reports, demonstrations, or presentations prepared by each of its members. In the middle school, teachers may ask groups to compile a single written report that reflects the entire group's research. Students can be asked to maintain a "unit portfolio" which includes samples of their individual written work, art projects, and other materials, such as a log or journal reflecting on their experiences during the unit of study.

Evaluating the Research-Oriented Thematic Unit

To conclude a research-oriented thematic unit, as a part of the evaluation process, teachers may want to prepare an examination based on notes generated from the committee reports. Each committee can be asked to develop several questions about its work. The questions can then be used for a review of concepts developed in the unit; after careful editing by the teacher, some committee questions might become part of a final examination.

The decision about which of the two unit types—*thematic* or *research-oriented thematic*—is more appropriate for a particular class should be based on the teacher's perception of the students' developmental and academic abilities. The organizational structure of a particular school will also influence that decision; this will be especially important if the school uses a departmentalized plan.

The steps in creating each of the two unit designs described above will be explained further and illustrated in chapters 5 and 6. Chapter 6 also offers a plan that may facilitate the use of research-oriented thematic units in departmentalized situations.

References

Arends, R. (1995). *Learning to teach* (3rd ed.). New York: McGraw-Hill.

Berk, L. E. (1996). *Infants, children, and adolescents* (2nd ed.). Boston: Allyn & Bacon.

Bruner, J. (1990). *Acts of meaning.* Cambridge, MA: Harvard University Press.

Case, R. (1985). *Intellectual development: Birth to adulthood.* Orlando, FL: Academic Press.

Dembo, M. (1988). *Applying educational psychology in the classroom* (3rd ed.). New York: Longman.

Flavell, J. H. (1985). *Cognitive development* (2nd ed.). Upper Saddle River, NJ: Prentice Hall.

Forman, E. A., Minick, N., & Stone, C. A. (1993). *Contexts for learning.* New York: Oxford University Press.

Furth, H. G. (1971). *Piaget for teachers.* Upper Saddle River, NJ: Prentice Hall.

Gardner, H. (1991). *The unschooled mind: How children think and how schools should teach.* New York: Basic Books.

Gardner, H. (1993). *Multiple intelligences: The theory in practice.* New York: Basic Books.

Gardner, H. (1995, January 6). Creating creativity. *The Times Educational Supplement,* No. 4097, p. 15.

Kauchak, D., & Eggen, P. (1989). *Learning and teaching.* Boston: Allyn & Bacon.

NCSS Task Force. (1989). Social studies for early childhood and elementary school children preparing for the 21st century: A report from NCSS Task Force on Early Childhood/Elementary Social Studies. *Social Education, 53,* 14–23.

Phillips, J. (1981). *Piaget's theory: A primer.* San Francisco: W. H. Freeman.

Piaget, J. (1955). *The language and thought of the child.* New York: Meridian.

Piaget, J. (1966). *Judgment and reasoning in the child.* Totowa, NJ: Littlefield, Adams.

Piaget, J. (1970). *Science of education and the psychology of the child.* New York: Orion.

Piaget, J. (1973). *To understand is to invent.* New York: Grossman.

Piaget, J. (1974). *Understanding causality.* New York: W. W. Norton.

Piaget, J. (1976). *The grasp of consciousness.* Cambridge, MA: Harvard University Press.

Piaget, J., & Inhelder, B. (1969). *The psychology of the child.* New York: Basic Books.

Santrock, J. W. (1995). *Children* (4th ed.). Madison, WI: Brown & Benchmark.

Santrock, J. W. (1996). *Child development* (7th ed.). Madison, WI: Brown & Benchmark.

Slavin, R. (1995). *Cooperative learning.* New York: Longman.

Slavin, R., Sharan, S., Kagan, S., Hertz-Lazarowitz, R., Webb, C., & Schmuck, R. (Eds.). (1985). *Learning to cooperate, cooperating to learn.* New York: Plenum.

Vygotsky, L. S. (1986). *Thought and language.* Cambridge, MA: The MIT Press.

Wadsworth, B. (1996). *Piaget's theory of cognitive and affective development* (5th ed.). White Plains, NY: Longman.

Wertsch, J. V. (1985). *Vygotsky and the social formation of the mind.* Cambridge, MA: Harvard University Press.

Suggested Readings

The following readings can provide additional material on the main topic of this chapter, child development. The list includes general child development textbooks as well as a number of historically classic reports of research in the field. Several books address the relationships between development and instructional approaches.

Berk, L. E. (1994). *Infants and children: Prenatal through middle childhood.* Boston: Allyn & Bacon.

Brainerd, C. J. (1978). *Piaget's theory of intelligence.* Upper Saddle River, NJ: Prentice Hall.

Burke, D. L. (1995, Fall). The future now: A child-centered school mosaic. *Kappa Delta Pi Record, 53,* 23–27.

Charbonneau, M. P., & Reider, B. E. (1995). *The integrated elementary classroom: A developmental model of education for the 21st century.* Needham Heights, MA: Allyn & Bacon.

Cole, M., & Cole, S. R. (1993). *The development of children* (2nd ed.). New York: Scientific American.

Flavell, J. H., Green, F. L., & Flavell, E. R. (1995). *Young children's knowledge about thinking.* Chicago: Society for Research in Child Development, University of Chicago Press.

Forman, G. E., & Kuschner, D. S. (1977). *The child's construction of knowledge.* Monterey, CA: Brooks/Cole.

Furth, H. G. (1969). *Human development* (4th ed.). Upper Saddle River, NJ: Prentice Hall.

Furth, H. G., & Wachs, H. (1974). *Thinking goes to school.* New York: Oxford University Press.

Gardner, H. (1982). *Art, mind and brain: A cognitive approach to creativity.* New York: Basic Books.

Gardner, H. (1983). *Frames of mind: The theory of multiple intelligences.* New York: Basic Books.

Gardner, H. (1985). *The mind's new science: A history of the cognitive revolution.* New York: Basic Books.

Hersh, R. H., Paolitto, D. P., & Reinger, J. (1979). *Promoting moral growth: From Piaget to Kohlberg.* New York: Longman.

Holt, J. (1967). *How children learn.* New York: Pitman.

Paris, S. G., Olson, G. M., & Stevenson, H. W. (1993). *Learning and motivation in the classroom.* Hillsdale, NJ: Erlbaum.

Phillips, J. L. (1981). *Piaget's theory: A primer.* San Francisco: W. H. Freeman.

Santrock, J. W. (1995). *Children* (4th ed.). Dubuque, IA: Brown & Benchmark.

Sava, S. G. (1975). *Learning through discovery for young children.* New York: McGraw-Hill.

Schwebel, M., & Raph, J. (Eds.). (1973). *Piaget in the classroom.* New York: Basic Books.

Seifert, K. L., & Hoffnung, R. J. (1991). *Child and adolescent development* (2nd ed.). Boston: Houghton Mifflin.

Sigel, I. E., Grodzinsky, D. M., & Golinkoff, R. M. (1981). *New directions in Piagetian theory and practice.* Hillsdale, NJ: Erlbaum.

Torbert, W. R. (1972). *Learning from experience: Toward consciousness.* New York: Columbia University Press.

Vygotsky, L. S. (1986). *Thought and language* (new revised ed.). Cambridge, MA: MIT Press.

Wadsworth, B. J. (1978). *Piaget for the classroom teacher.* New York: Longman.

3

Teaching Requirements and Concerns

Chapter 3 reviews the following considerations of teachers who use interdisciplinary instruction:

- *A list of the primary requirements of teachers who plan to use an interdisciplinary approach in their classrooms.*
- *An overview of unit planning, learning principles, learning styles, team teaching, and technology in interdisciplinary education.*

···

*T*eachers who are convinced that other approaches to education can offer satisfactory substitutes for traditional programs find that they need to keep several teaching requirements and considerations in mind. It is, of course, important to take time to plan carefully, to think through any new processes, to consider the logistics associated with any methodological changes, and to consider the effects of any modifications in the instructional program. These concerns are especially important for teachers who plan to explore the interdisciplinary method as an alternative.

Requirements

General and Child Development Knowledge

First, in order to be secure with interdisciplinary methods, teachers need to bring a sizeable fund of general knowledge to their practice. Although teachers should encourage independence in students and avoid giving answers their students are able to find for themselves, a broad general knowledge base is an essential asset for guiding students through interdisciplinary studies.

Equally important, teachers need to have a thorough background in the area of human development and, what is equally important, the ability to apply their understandings about cognitive and affective development in practice. Certainly, an awareness of students' thinking and reasoning characteristics can help teachers tailor their instruction more effectively for students at different developmental levels.

Gardner's multiple intelligences theory was outlined in Chapter 2, and it was recommended that the intelligences need to be considered when planning thematic units. Gardner (1991) also indicates that his theory has implications for instruction. A practical resource for teachers, *Multiple Intelligences in the Classroom* (Armstrong, 1994), provides numerous helpful suggestions for designing lessons and activities that address each of the seven intelligences.

Another book is an important source for teachers who use interdisciplinary methods. *In Search of Understanding: The Case for Constructivist Classrooms* (Brooks & Brooks, 1993) relates contemporary developmental theory and classroom practice and provides teachers with alternatives to traditional textbook learning activities.

A Compatible Educational Philosophy

Another factor to be considered is the compatibility between a teacher's educational philosophy and interdisciplinary methodology. Kimpston, Williams, and Stockton (1992) show ways in which specific philosophies of education and teaching methods are related to one another. Their analysis indicates that the *experimentalist* and *reconstructionist* philosophies are more compatible with interdisciplinary methods than others. This is true mainly because both philosophies emphasize the importance of the learning processes. Teachers who subscribe to those philosophies are, therefore, more likely to feel comfortable with interdisciplinary instruction than teachers who do not. Explanations of experimentalism and reconstructionism can be found in most educational foundations textbooks. Ozman and Craver (1995) and Duck (1981) provide especially clear presentations of educational philosophies and discuss their effects on the teaching process.

Classroom Management Skills

Classroom management is a serious matter for every teacher; certainly orchestrating a well-run classroom requires expert organization, planning, scheduling, and behavioral management skills. Clearly, a teacher's ability to plan for instruction is directly related to success in classroom management. Interdisciplinary instruction requires teachers to develop special skills in planning comprehensive instructional units as well as lessons that interest and involve children and provide the guidance they need to pursue their inquiries. In the primary grades, unit planning demands ingenuity at generating lessons and activities related to central themes of units the children study. Students in the intermediate grades and middle school are able to undertake more sophisticated forms of research, making it important for their teachers to have a thorough understanding of research processes. Therefore, in addition to being good organizers, teachers who use interdisciplinary methods need to be skillful planners.

A great deal of activity usually occurs during the development of an interdisciplinary unit when it is often necessary to manage several different activities at the same time. Because both formal and informal work periods are needed in unit work, teachers need to be flexible and willing to adapt to the unique types and levels of activity that arise. At the same time, teachers have to be sensitive to the often subtle difference between activities that are productive and those that are potentially chaotic.

Many authoritative sources are available for teachers that provide information on a number of well-known behavioral management research designs and models, such as those by Putnam and Burke (1992); Osborn and Osborn (1989); Valentine (1987); Charles (1983); Barr, Dreeben, and Wiratchai (1983); and Jones and Jones (1981). Each text reviews management models that can help to improve student behavior and suggests effective ways to discipline students. The models are not discussed here; instead, several common suggestions are offered, which may be especially helpful for teachers who are just beginning their careers. Many experienced teachers have found that the following suggestions can help to improve classroom behavior and maintain a healthy emotional classroom climate for interdisciplinary instruction.

Maintain a Professional Approach to Discipline

Set an example for students by being polite to them. Discipline privately and avoid embarrassing students. Avoid showing anger, and be brief, but firm, when administering corrective measures. A professional way for teachers to gain insights about individual students' attitudes and feelings—and perhaps some problematic behaviors—is to have students maintain journals that are used for private communications between student and teacher. Johnston (1992) suggests that in these daily journal entries, "Students and teacher have a context in which they can write about things that are bothering them in the classroom and they can communicate about them in a reflective way" (p. 139).

Encourage Students to Become Invested in Their Classroom

At the beginning of a new school year, when teachers are especially hopeful of establishing good rapport with their students, many intend to offer a hearty welcome by preparing beautiful, artistic displays that cover the classroom. Students who enter a meticulous, teacher-prepared classroom may feel that, because the room has been so well decorated by their teacher, it is not really *their* room, nor is maintaining it primarily *their* responsibility. The students may feel that because everything has already been done, they will not need to contribute or be invited to participate. Therefore, it might be wiser for teachers to encourage the children to become involved in deciding how the room should be decorated. Certainly, there are many decisions in which students can participate. Interdisciplinary units of study offer some of those opportunities. For example, students can suggest titles for their interdisciplinary units; they can prepare bulletin boards, create murals, and display their art and construction projects.

Perhaps if students are involved in these and other ways in their classrooms, they will feel that the classroom is theirs as well as their teacher's. In turn, they may also be motivated to care for it better because they have an *investment* in it. In fact, "Children should be made to feel that they own the classroom and should take responsibility for its uses as well as contribute suggestions concerning its organization" (Pappas, Kiefer, & Levstik, 1995, p. 66).

Make Expectations of Appropriate Behavior Clear

Usually, students have a good general idea about what is and is not appropriate behavior. It is evident that children know what the rules should be whenever they are asked to participate in deciding classroom rules at the beginning of a school year. Nonetheless, most students will test any teacher to determine what is acceptable in his or her classroom, and they look to their teacher to be the key person in setting behavior standards.

Be Consistent with the Kinds of Behavior You Expect

Students expect their teachers to be fair. In fact, children will often behave inappropriately to show their resentment of teachers who are unfair.

Be an Aware Person

Let students know that you are aware of what is happening in the classroom. Students look to their teachers for guidance; therefore, they expect teachers to exercise authority, provide clear directions, and have reasonable expectations, both for their behavior and academic work. In order to provide the kind of guidance needed, teachers have to be constantly aware of all that is happening in the room, and the students need to know that their teachers are always *tuned-in*.

Maintain Physical Proximity by Being Among Students

Simply walking closer to a student who is not behaving well can let the student know you are aware of what the student is doing. Proximity alone can often correct a minor problem, such as occasional off-task behavior or failure to share responsibilities in a committee or cooperative group activity.

Consider All Problem Situations in Their Context

Try not to overreact. This is especially important when rules are broken or the students who usually behave well suddenly present a problem. At those times, it is important for teachers to analyze each situation before reacting. Factors, such as the weather, the day of the week, the time of day and time of year—particularly preholiday seasons and the late spring months near the end of the school year—can stimulate some unusual behavior.

Teachers who keep their perspective when problems arise may even find that some situations will offer opportunities to convey the importance of classroom rules, helping to reestablish order.

Expect the Unexpected

Planning carefully will usually help teachers to be better prepared when something goes awry during a lesson or activity—when a student responds with an unusual or unanticipated answer or when a student suddenly interrupts. At those times, it is especially important to be prepared for the spontaneous shifts or changes that may be necessary as a teaching session continues. Of course, unexpected events that arise when teaching can be disconcerting, but they can also be informative, even refreshing to both teachers and students.

Teachers cannot and would probably not want to prevent any surprises from ever arising during an instructional session. It is therefore important to be as ready for them as possible and not to be discouraged when they do.

Recognize That Individual Students May Require Different Approaches or Different Kinds of Help

In a healthy emotional classroom environment, it is usually only a few students who need constant reminding about their behavior. Although the goal should always be to help students learn to control their own behavior, teachers may need, at least temporarily, to accept responsibility for students who are not able or willing to control themselves.

Be Inventive in the Ways You Handle Annoying Behaviors, Such as Complaining and Tattling

For example, teachers can ask students who are complaining about one another to write out their complaints before attempting to make any judgments. Sometimes complaints seem less important to students after they take the time to write about them. Ellis (1995) recommends that teachers have students solve classroom management problems by applying the same inquiry skills they would use to investigate other problems. This keeps the focus on "solutions rather than sources of blame" (p. 349).

The preceding list is only a small sample of suggestions that can help teachers establish the kind of healthy emotional climate needed for managing student classroom behavior.

Instructional Concerns

Unit Planning

Planning interdisciplinary units requires considerable professional skill; poorly planned units generally resemble an assortment of loosely connected lessons that lack a central theme. Jacobs (1989) has referred to this kind of unit planning as the "potpourri approach." Teachers are likely to be disappointed with the results of units that are unfocused; they may even be discouraged from undertaking other interdisciplinary units as a result.

In addition to unit planning skills, interdisciplinary units often make use of every instructional mode: working with the whole class, small cooperative groups, and individuals. Therefore, teachers need to develop techniques for working with those modes. More specific information on planning and teaching thematic and research-oriented thematic units will be provided in chapters 4, 5, and 6.

Principles of Learning

Successful teachers always attend to major knowledge acquisition and learning principles. Those principles are central to Piaget's (1963) adaptation theory, and Wakefield (1993) offers a strong supportive argument for attending to them in her discussion of developmentally appropriate teaching practices. Kamii (1973) also provides a detailed discussion of the relevance of specific pedagogical principles based on Piagetian theory. Several of those principles are especially significant for interdisciplinary instruction:

- As learners mature, they construct their own knowledge through personal experience and social interaction with others.

- In order to be adapted, new knowledge must build on a learner's existing knowledge base.

- Intrinsic motivation is more effective than extrinsic forms of motivation.
- Unified, thematic studies help to clarify connections among the various academic disciplines.
- Learning processes—learning how to learn—are important in all academic instruction.

Individual Learning Styles

Today, any list of important teaching concerns must include attention to children's individual styles of learning. Although learning styles may be defined differently by various authorities, most agree that the term **learning styles** refers to the unique, individual strengths, preferences, and approaches students tend to have as they attempt to acquire knowledge. Teachers, therefore, need to plan instruction for their classes so that it coincides with the ways students are able to learn best.

Because learning styles will not be discussed in detail in this book, readers are referred to other especially informative sources. Howard Gardner, whose work on multiple intelligences has already been cited in this book (1991, 1993), is one of the foremost contemporary researchers in the field of developmental psychology. Gardner has provided us with evidence to support his theory that identifying students' individual cognitive strengths, individual *working styles*, will enable more students to succeed in school. At the same time, Gardner expresses his desire that his theory not be misinterpreted and that teachers seek appropriate applications of the theory in their classrooms (Viadero, 1995).

In a collection of 23 articles on learning styles, written by an interdisciplinary group of professionals, we find different interpretations of learning styles (Learning Styles, 1990). Additional works provide other ways of looking at learning styles, ways to diagnose them, and methods for teaching students in accord with their individual styles (Kagan, 1987; Phye & Andre, 1986; Fizzell, 1984; O'Neil & Spielberger, 1979; Dunn & Dunn, 1978).

Team Teaching and Interdisciplinary Instruction

Numerous opportunities are presented for collaboration among teachers who use the interdisciplinary method. Classroom teachers need to work cooperatively with special area teachers: art, music, and physical education teachers, special education specialists, the school nurse, and perhaps others in the school environment. Specialists need to be contacted in advance of initiating any unit, so they will be able to plan lessons and activities that coincide with and contribute to the unit theme.

This type of collaborative work among the teachers will help students discover the relevance of the social sciences, science, the arts, music, health, and other special areas to the themes they study. Cooperation between the classroom teacher and specialists is a form of team teaching that can contribute significantly to ensuring the interdisciplinary quality of thematic units.

Observing special area teachers over time, classroom teachers develop knowledge of the processes that specialists use with children. For example, an art teacher may reserve a class period for instructing children in a papier-mâché project. After observing the process followed by the specialist, the classroom teacher may be able to use it without help in the future.

Of course, team teaching is not restricted to cooperative work with specialists. In some middle schools, interdepartmental teams are organized. A three-teacher interdepartmental team might consist, for example, of a social studies teacher, an English or language arts teacher, and an art specialist. The team is assigned a block of time to work with a group of students, and teachers have a scheduled time for planning purposes. Together, they design the interdisciplinary units they teach and decide how to allocate the time in their block; they each plan to relate their lessons to the unit theme as much as possible. Sometimes, students are included in the planning sessions as well; this kind of student participation in the planning process has been found to have considerable value in interdisciplinary instruction (Stevenson & Carr, 1993).

An alternative way to organize for interdisciplinary instruction in a departmental structure will be discussed in Chapter 6. Readers are also referred to two discussions that specifically address concerns of middle school teachers who are involved in teaming arrangements (Williamson, 1993; Vars, 1969).

In schools having self-contained classes, another teaming plan may be arranged. This structure usually involves two or more teachers who combine their classes and work cooperatively with the larger group of children. Under this plan, each of the teachers may have a special area of expertise to offer the larger group. At times, the teachers rotate serving as the main instructor while others assist; however, they are all involved in teaching skills and processes. Similar to interdepartmental plans, teachers on a self-contained team have time reserved in their regular teaching schedule to plan together and to share their knowledge of individual children's progress. Interacting in this way helps keep team members abreast of children's interests, strengths, and limitations.

Both interdepartmental and self-contained team teaching arrangements are compatible with interdisciplinary instruction, and they are based on sound child development principles. Because team members work together as a unit, instruction can be unified and genuinely interdisciplinary rather than fragmented or divided into separate and unrelated disciplinary studies.

Some organizational structures may actually inhibit interdisciplinary instruction because they fragment the curriculum and, in fact, isolate teachers from one another. For example, totally departmentalized instruction and modified Joplin plan arrangements do not usually provide for genuine *team* teaching. In a departmentalized structure, children change classes for instruction in the various disciplines at appointed times throughout the day. The modified Joplin plan involves exchanging classes at a particular grade level and grouping children homogeneously for skills instruction in some subject areas during a part of the day.

Both structures rarely afford teachers scheduled time to plan together or to exchange information on the progress of individual children. The interrelationships among disciplines tend to be obscured when reading is taught only by the reading teacher, mathematics is taught only during a mathematics lesson, and all subjects are taught in isolation from one another.

Technology

No list of instructional concerns would be complete without mentioning the burgeoning use of technology in our schools. Telecommunications via the computer and interactive computer software programs are rapidly becoming essential tools for students and teachers.

Many elementary and middle schools are now connected to networking services, joining classrooms and schools with one another, with colleges and universities, and with the Internet. Online services devoted to educational purposes allow students to investigate topics individually, in cooperative learning groups within their own classrooms, and/or with students in other schools. Examples of such services are the National Geographic Society's *Kids Network*, the *International Education and Resource Network*, and *New York Link Learning Link.*

New York Link Learning Link is an example of a commercial online network for teachers and students in kindergarten through grade 12; the service is available throughout New York State and in selected sites in other parts of the United States. In one of New York Link Learning Link's most valuable services, called "classroom exchanges," predesigned interdisciplinary problems are offered to interested classes at three general levels: grades 2 to 4, 4 to 6, and 7 to 12. After a problem is outlined, students first work in their own classrooms using their usual resources to research the problem. Then, using the online service, they are able to compare notes, raise questions, and discuss their ideas and findings with other classes working on the same problem.

Using computers, students can conduct searches and investigate problems with many exceptional interactive CD-ROM programs and interdisciplinary multimedia reference resources, including such well-known programs as *Rain Forest, Oregon Trail,* and *Where in the World Is Carmen San Diego?* While conducting their inquiries, students can develop their own time lines—in either English or Spanish—with *Timeliner,* distributed by Tom Snyder Productions, Inc. Comprehensive CD-ROM dictionaries, thesauruses, atlases, and encyclopedias are readily available. Students can also learn to use databases and spreadsheets to help them organize information using software produced by Claris Works and other companies. In addition to using the computer to search for information, students can use word processing programs to take notes and write papers and letters, send and receive e-mail, and use desktop publishing facilities.

Resources for Teachers

Using local online services and the Internet, teachers can exchange lesson and unit plans with other professionals throughout the country and can interact with groups of interested teachers. One of the most helpful references on the Internet for teachers and parents is *Brave New Schools* (Cummins & Sayers, 1995). In their book, the authors explain in detail how to access the Internet, they discuss some of its valuable resources for students, and give directions on locating sources of information. E-mail and Internet addresses are included for the sources, saving teachers much valuable time.

Teachers can prepare special materials, such as slide shows, to integrate with other teaching tools in presenting their lessons. Digital cameras can be used to record videos of students' oral reports and other presentations to add to their assessment portfolios. Local telecommunications groups, such as the United Federation of Teachers *New York City Teacher Centers Consortium*, give teachers access to technical and instructional assistance to help them integrate the computer and other technology in their teaching.

In addition to materials for students, some software companies have also produced thematic units for teachers to use or adapt. Good Apple, a company based in Carthage, Illinois, has several interdisciplinary units specifically for young children. New York Times Educational Media, located in Newtown, Pennsylvania, has published a series of modules on themes suited to older groups in the middle and secondary school. Sunburst Communications, in Pleasantville, New York, has already produced numerous programs in nearly every discipline for students at all age levels. This company is also responsible for a well-known interdisciplinary unit, the *Voyage of the Mimi*, a plan that includes guidebooks for teachers as well as accompanying materials for students.

Educational television is also playing a revived and important role in many areas. For example, in New York City, the local PBS television station, WNET, airs numerous educational programs for students at all grade levels. These programs are broadcast from 2:00 A.M. to 5:00 A.M. for teachers to videotape and use in their classrooms. Copyright privileges are arranged by the television station so that teachers are free to videotape and use the programs with their students. A complete guide to all programs to be aired each academic year is available from the station at a nominal cost. The guide includes a topical reference and complete descriptions of each program. Similar services may be available in other cities.

Educational television, computer programs, and telecommunications will supplement, not replace, other media. Teachers who plan to use interdisciplinary instruction will continue to use conventional audiovisual materials: videotape recorders, monitors, film and filmstrip projectors, overhead projectors, and tape recorders. Newer equipment, such as LCD projectors, should rapidly become standard in schools as well.

References

Armstrong, T. (1994). *Multiple intelligences in the classroom*. Alexandria, VA: Association for Supervision and Curriculum Development.

Barr, R., Dreeben, R., & Wiratchai, N. (1983). *How schools work*. Chicago: University of Chicago Press.

Bright, G. W. (1987). *Microcomputer applications in the elementary classroom: A guide for teachers*. Needham Heights, MA: Allyn & Bacon.

Brooks, J. G., & Brooks, M. G. (1993). *In search of understanding: The case for constructivist classrooms.* Alexandria, VA: Association for Supervision and Curriculum Development.

Charles, C. M. (1983). *Elementary classroom management.* New York: Longman.

Cummins, J., & Sayers, D. (1995). *Brave new schools.* New York: St. Martin's Press.

Diem, R. A. (1989). Instructional applications for computers: The next step. *Kappa Delta Pi Record, 25*(2), 60–62.

Duck, L. (1981). *Teaching with charisma.* Boston: Allyn & Bacon.

Dunn, R., & Dunn, K. (1978). *Teaching students through their individual learning styles.* Reston, VA: Reston Publishers.

Ellis, A. K. (1995). *Teaching and learning elementary social studies* (5th ed.). Boston: Allyn & Bacon.

Fizzell, R. (1984). The status of learning styles. *The Educational Forum, 48*(3), 303–12.

Gardner, H. (1983). *Frames of mind: The theory of multiple intelligences.* New York: Basic Books.

Gardner, H. (1991). *The unschooled mind: How children think and how schools should teach.* New York: Basic Books.

Gardner, H. (1993). *Multiple intelligences: The theory in practice.* New York: Basic Books.

Jacobs, H. (Ed.). (1989). *Interdisciplinary curriculum: Design and implementation.* Alexandria, VA: Association for Supervision and Curriculum Development.

Johnston, P. H. (1992). *Constructive evaluation of literate activity.* White Plains, NY: Longman.

Jones, V. & Jones, L. (1981). *Responsible classroom discipline.* Boston: Allyn & Bacon.

Kagan, D. (1987). Cognitive style and instructional preferences: Some inferences. *The Educational Forum, 51*(4), 393–403.

Kamii, C. (1973). Pedagogical principles derived from Piaget's theory: Relevance for educational practice. In M. Schwebel & J. Raph (Eds.), *Piaget in the classroom.* New York: Basic.

Kimpston, R., Williams, H., & Stockton, W. (Winter, 1992). Ways of knowing and the curriculum. *The Educational Forum, 56*(2), 153–72.

Kleiman, G. M. (1985). *Brave new schools: How computers can change education.* Needham Heights, MA: Allyn & Bacon.

Learning styles and the brain. (1990). *Educational Leadership, 48*(2), 4–81.

O'Neil, H. F., & Spielberger, C. D. (1979). *Cognitive and affective learning strategies.* New York: Academic Press.

Osborn, D. K., & Osborn, J. (1989). *Discipline and classroom management* (3rd ed.). Athens, GA: Daye.

Ozman, H. L., & Craver, S. (1995). *Philosophical foundations of education* (5th ed.). Upper Saddle River, NJ: Merrill/Prentice Hall.

Pappas, C. C., Kiefer, B. Z., & Levstik, L. S. (1995). *An integrated language perspective in the elementary school.* White Plains, NY: Longman.

Phye, G. D., & Andre, T. (1986). *Cognitive classroom learning.* Orlando, FL: Academic Press.

Piaget, J. (1963). *Judgment and reasoning in the child.* Totowa, NJ: Littlefield, Adams.

Piaget, J. (1969). *Science of education and the psychology of the child.* New York: Orion.

Piaget, J. (1974). *Understanding causality.* New York: W. W. Norton.

Piaget, J., & Inhelder, B. (1975). *The origin of the idea of chance in children.* New York: W. W. Norton.

Putnam, J. G., & Burke, J. B. (1992). *Organizing and managing classroom learning communities.* New York: McGraw-Hill.

Stevenson, C., & Carr, J. F. (1993). *Integrated studies in the middle grades.* New York: Teachers College Press.

Valentine, M. R. (1987). *How to deal with discipline problems.* Dubuque, IA: Kendall/Hunt.

Vars, G. F. (1969). *Common learnings; core and interdisciplinary team approaches.* Scranton, PA: International Textbook.

Viadero, D. (1995, November 8). Expert testimony. *Education Week*, pp. 33–34.

Wakefield, A. (1993). Developmentally appropriate practice: Figuring things out. *The Educational Forum, 57*(2), 134–45.

Williamson, R. (1993). *Scheduling the middle level school to meet early adolescent needs.* Reston, VA: National Association of Secondary School Principals.

Suggested Readings

The supplemental readings listed below provide additional background material for the concerns discussed in this chapter, including development, classroom management, learning styles, principles of learning, philosophy, team teaching, and technology.

Frowzier, H. W. (1985). Microcomputers in schools. *The Educational Forum, 50*(1), 87–100.

Hanslovsky, G., Moyer, S., & Wagner, H. (1969). *Why team teaching?* Columbus, OH: Merrill.

Holt, J. (1967). *How children learn.* New York: Pitman.

Holt, J. (1989). *Learning all the time.* Reading, MA: Addison-Wesley.

Kindsvatter, R., & Wilen, W. (1992). *Dynamics of effective teaching* (2nd ed.). White Plains, NY: Longman.

Knirk, F. G., & Gustafson, K. L. (1986). *Instructional technology: A systematic approach to education.* New York: Holt, Rinehart & Winston.

Palardy, J. M. (Ed.). (1983). *Elementary education: An anthology of trends and issues.* Lanham, MD: University Press of America.

Paris, S. G., Olson, G. M., & Stevenson, H. W. (1993). *Learning and motivation in the classroom.* Hillsdale, NJ: Erlbaum.

Peterson, D. (Ed.). (1984). *Intelligent schoolhouse: Readings on computers and learning.* Reston, VA: Reston.

Posner, M. (1994). *HEL internet guide.* Cambridge, MA: Harvard Graduate School of Education.

Ramsden, P. (Ed.). (1988). *Improving learning.* London: Kogan Page.

Sadowski, M. (1995). Moving beyond traditional subjects requires teachers to abandon their 'comfort zones.' *The Harvard Education Letter, 11*(5), 1–5.

Sigel, I. E., Grodzinsky, D. M., & Golinkoff, R. M. (1981). *New directions in Piagetian theory and practice.* Hillsdale, NJ: Erlbaum.

Stensrud, R., & Stensrud, K. (1981). Discipline: An attitude, not an outcome. *The Educational Forum, 45*(2), 161–168.

Wadsworth, B. J. (1978). *Piaget for the classroom teacher.* New York: Longman.

Wadsworth, B. J. (1996). *Piaget's theory of cognitive and affective development* (5th ed.). White Plains, NY: Longman.

Woronov, R. (1994, September/October). Six myths (and five promising truths) about the uses of educational technology. *The Harvard Education Letter, 10*(5), 1–3.

4

Preliminary Steps in the Unit Planning Process

Chapter 4 provides information about the interdisciplinary unit planning process and reviews general planning strategies used in connection with that process. Specifically, the chapter includes:

- *A review of two developmentally appropriate methods for selecting themes for interdisciplinary units.*
- *A practical unit plan design that may be especially helpful for teachers who are learning to plan interdisciplinary units.*
- *A review of general planning strategies needed when developing interdisciplinary unit plans. These strategies include preparing instructional objectives, developing questions, using Bloom's Taxonomy to determine levels of instruction, evaluating children's unit work, and planning learning centers.*

*W*hen teachers first begin to plan and teach interdisciplinary units in their classes, there are often two questions on their minds. The first concerns where to find ideas for the themes to be taught at their grade levels, and the second question deals with the design and development of the written unit plan. Experienced teachers have found ways to approach these two tasks.

Selecting Interdisciplinary Themes

Teachers who are new to the interdisciplinary method will want to know how to select suitable themes for their units. Two developmentally based approaches to this task are followed by publishers of elementary social studies textbooks and can be observed in the state syllabi that teachers find useful when selecting themes for their units.

In the first, the **widening horizons** strategy, themes are ordered according to children's developmental levels. Children initially study themes that are within their personal experience and about which they have some prior knowledge. In the primary grades, for example, themes begin with the study of self and family; later, children study their school and neighborhood. Regions, states, nations, and cultures in the eastern and western hemispheres are studied by older groups. To use the widening horizons approach in selecting social themes for a particular grade level, teachers can usually rely on those listed in science and social studies textbooks and the state syllabi.

Some educators have criticized the exclusive use of the widening horizons strategy to select themes for interdisciplinary units. Ravich (1988), for example, feels that by following the widening horizons approach, students will be limited to simple, familiar themes that may fail to challenge or motivate them. This is a reasonable concern today when, even before they enter school, many young children have been exposed to so much information via television and other media. However, if teachers keep this possible limitation in mind when selecting their themes, the widening horizons approach can still serve as a useful general guide.

The second approach to selecting themes involves the development of concepts. In Bruner's **spiraling curriculum,** children may be exposed to the same social science concepts at every grade level (1963). Each year, new and more complex aspects of those concepts are introduced as children become developmentally ready to understand them. For example, the concept "community" can be taught at each grade. As children become intellectually ready, they are exposed to more sophisticated meanings of that concept. Bruner's approach is compatible with and can complement the widening horizons strategy; whereas the widening horizons approach centers on the selection of *topics*, the spiral curriculum involves developing broad *concepts.*

It is clear in the preceding descriptions that both the widening horizons and spiraling curriculum strategies take into consideration important child development characteristics. Other factors are also important in the selection of themes. For example, thought should be given to students' academic skills—especially their skill levels in reading, writing and research. Students' interests and their ability to work together also need to be considered.

Several practical matters also influence the selection process. The availability of sufficient supplies of appropriate learning resource materials for a theme is critically important. Not only books, but other media resources will be needed to investigate most themes. These resources include children's magazines and newspapers, relevant films, filmstrips, video presentations, computer software programs, and computer networking possibilities. Teachers need to know that students will have the equipment and materials needed for related constructions, art projects, and science experiments. For a detailed description of the thinking process a group of teachers working together might experience as they select a unit theme, the reader is referred to Perkins's interesting, informative scenario on this important task (Jacobs, 1989, pp. 67–76).

Once a theme has been chosen, the final decision to make concerns the *type* of unit plan to be designed. Because there are substantial differences between thematic and research-oriented thematic units, and because each type of unit and its planning format have attributes tailored both to students' developmental levels and their academic skills, teachers need to decide which of the two unit plan types is more appropriate for the theme and the students with whom they are working.

Interdisciplinary Unit Plan Design

Most teaching methods textbooks include unit plan outlines. However, perusal of those textbooks, including books on the teaching of science and social studies, reveals that there is no consensus about a unit plan format among the different authors. For example, the emphasis in one text may be on unit objectives, another mainly lists resources, while still another may suggest that units are simply a collection of lesson plans.

The unit plan format recommended here is primarily a description of *ideas* for possible lessons and activities related to a central theme to be studied by a group of children. This design is similar to the theme studies described by Charbonneau and Reider (1995) and the unit plan model in Jacobs's text (1989). Each time the same unit is retaught, complete plans for the lessons and activities that are actually used can be added to the initial unit plan design. Thus, the unit plan is perceived as a dynamic, constantly changing, ever-developing record.

Whenever a teacher or teaching team designs a new unit—one that has not been taught before—it is unnecessary to write detailed plans for all the lessons and activities suggested in the plan. The reason for delaying the detailed planning for most lessons is simply to conserve a teacher's planning time. Often, after the unit is introduced, it will be decided that some lessons or activities should be eliminated or that they are not appropriate for that particular group of children. Even though complete lesson plans need not be prepared initially, brief descriptions of those lessons or activities should be included in a separate section of the unit plan. The descriptions include the general idea and purpose of each lesson or activity idea. Complete lesson plans can then be prepared from those descriptions if and when they are needed as the unit progresses.

At first, only one lesson or activity, the one that will introduce the unit, will have to be prepared in detail. In the initial lesson, students will begin responding to the unit theme, and their special interests and needs will begin to surface. Their reactions during the first lesson can make it easier for the teacher to decide which of the possible lesson and activity ideas in the unit plan will be most appropriate to include as the study develops. Then, only the lessons and activities actually selected to be taught will need to be planned completely.

In its initial design, therefore, an interdisciplinary unit plan of either type— a thematic or research-oriented thematic unit—will have only one fully developed lesson plan, the one to be used to introduce the unit. The introductory lesson plan in a research-oriented thematic unit is as important as it is in a thematic unit because it begins the critical planning phase in the research process.

Chapters 5 and 6 will provide detailed guidelines illustrating specific steps to follow when designing each type of interdisciplinary unit. Several general planning strategies will be discussed here, including: writing instructional objectives; raising questions of different types; using Bloom's Taxonomy to determine the cognitive levels of objectives, directions, and questions; evaluating students' work; and, finally, planning learning centers.

General Planning Strategies

Preparing Instructional Objectives

Interdisciplinary unit plans include two types of instructional objectives: **general objectives (or unit goals)** and **specific objectives.** The first type, general objectives, applies to overall purposes of a lesson or an entire unit of work. General objectives suggest broad-based or long-term goals toward which a unit or lesson can contribute in some specified ways. Relatively few general objectives can be addressed in a single lesson, and they can be stated in rather general ways.

There are three categories of *general* objectives in unit planning: content (or cognitive), attitudinal (or affective), and process objectives. Three examples follow:

> To help increase students' understanding of the ways their government functions. *(general content objective)*
>
> To aid in developing a positive attitude about failure in scientific experimentation. *(general attitudinal objective)*
>
> To provide students with additional opportunities to practice the research process. *(general process objective)*

Specific objectives differ from general objectives in that they are short-term objectives that are included only in lesson and activity plans, mainly to provide a measure by which to assess the effectiveness of instruction. They usually follow a specific written form—a *behavioral* format. Below are three questions a teacher can ask that will help in formulating a behavioral objective:

*   What should the children learn (gain) from this lesson?

    This is the teacher's purpose or the informal objective the teacher keeps in mind while planning the procedure for the lesson.

*   How will the children show that they have met the objective of the lesson? What will they have to be able to *do?*

*   How well are the children expected to master this learning? *How well* will they need to perform what they are required to do?

Behavioral objective statements state (1) *for whom* the lesson is planned, (2) *what behavior* will indicate that students have met the objective the teacher had in mind, (3) the special *conditions* (if any) under which the behavior should be performed, and (4) *how well* the students must perform to successfully meet the objective. Examples of three behavioral objectives follow:

> After a trip to the zoo *(describes a condition)*, the children *(tells for whom the objective is intended)* will each complete a drawing of one animal observed at the zoo and dictate a sentence to be written by the teacher at the bottom of the picture telling at least one fact about the animal that was gained as a result of the field trip *(explains the specific behaviors to be demonstrated by the children)*.
>
> *The degree of acceptable performance in this objective for kindergarten or early first grade level is implied to be 100 percent.*
>
> Given a compass and five written directions to follow *(the conditions)*, each student *(for whom the objective is intended)* will accurately follow four of the five directions *(the behavior to be demonstrated and degree of acceptable performance; intermediate grade level)*.
>
> After a unit on "Emerging African Nations" *(the condition)*, the students *(for whom the objective is intended)* will pass a comprehensive unit test on major concepts developed in the unit *(the behavior to be demonstrated)* with at least 75 percent accuracy *(the degree of acceptable performance; middle school level)*.

To learn more about instructional objectives, readers are referred to a number of books in which the preparation of behavioral objectives is explained in detail. Several excellent references include those by Dembo (1988), Gronlund (1985), Mager (1984), Dick and Carey (1978), Davies (1976), and Kibler (1974).

Determining Cognitive Levels of Instruction Using Bloom's Taxonomy

Teachers prepare instructional objectives and raise questions at a variety of levels, from questions that elicit fundamental factual information to those requiring higher level, critical thinking on the part of students. Perhaps the most widely recognized classification system to help determine cognitive levels of objectives and questions is the one that was developed by Benjamin Bloom in 1956. Bloom outlined a six-level taxonomy to help teachers determine the relative difficulty of their instructional objectives, questions, directions, and test items. A brief outline of Bloom's Taxonomy follows:

Level 1: Knowledge

Questions at this basic level require students to provide simple, factual responses. Actual understanding may or may not be demonstrated in their answers. Questions at this level often stress memory, and they are generally convergent.

Examples

What is the name of the largest city on the west coast of the United States?

What is the meaning of the word "irrigation"?

Level 2: Comprehension

Understanding is required at this level. In response to questions at the comprehension level, students may be asked to explain, summarize, translate, and give examples to demonstrate their understanding.

Examples

Write a summary of the main points in this article.

Can someone explain how an irrigation system works in a desert area?

Level 3: Application

Students are required to use processes, problem solving, and research skills to determine their responses at this level of the taxonomy.

Examples

Now that you have recorded the daily temperature on this graph for the past three weeks, what does the record appear to indicate?

Can you sort these rocks into the three classifications we have just studied?

Level 4: Analysis

Analysis requires some interpretation, noting inferences, thinking beyond the literal level when reading, detecting cause-and-effect relationships, and drawing conclusions.

Examples

Let's try to figure out why our experiment with plants failed.

What reason can you give for the boy's actions in this story?

Level 5: Synthesis

Questions and directions for students at this level often ask for creative responses. New or original thinking is required to produce plans, raise hypotheses, predict, or produce original proposals, designs, art, or music.

Examples

Devise a plan that will help to minimize the effects of the increasing number of people who are settling in desert areas today.

Write a poem of your own that shows how you feel in the spring.

Level 6: Evaluation

Students make judgments at this level. They decide ratings and express opinions based on some standard or personal criteria.

Examples

Do you find that this essay on desert life includes accurate information about current problems in the lives of people who live there?

Which of these two plans to save endangered animals is better, or more likely to be effective?

Questioning

Successful planning at all levels also involves the development of important questioning strategies. Teachers need to become skilled at formulating both **convergent** and **divergent** questions. Convergent questions generally require a relatively narrow range of responses from students, while divergent questions are relatively open-ended and often encourage students to be creative in their answers. Models of the two question types are shown in Figures 4.1 and 4.2.

FIGURE 4.1
A convergent question and
response pattern

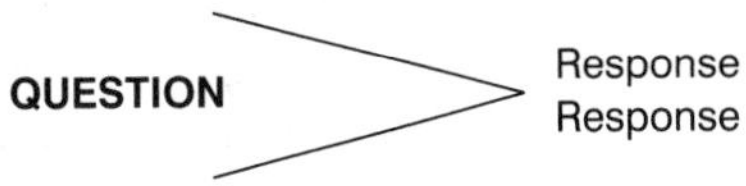

QUESTION > Response
Response

FIGURE 4.2
A divergent question and
response pattern

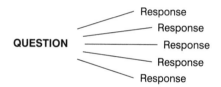

Examples (convergent questions)

Can you name two treaties that have involved European nations during the last two centuries?

Please define an amphibian.

Examples (divergent questions)

Can you think of a way to improve our local system of mass transit?

How did you feel when you listened to the recording of "Appalachian Spring"?

Evaluating Children's Unit Work

Evaluation is always an essential component of interdisciplinary instruction. Although educators agree that some form of assessment is needed, not all agree on the best ways to evaluate student progress. Ellis (1995) urges us to remember that because we cannot be certain that any one approach to evaluation is better than others, it is important for teachers to be familiar with several.

Traditionally, examinations and quizzes have been used more than any other evaluation tool. Most paper-and-pencil tests, however, are limited to assessing students' verbal and logical-mathematical achievement. To limit evaluation to formal and informal tests fails to recognize the value of the evaluation *process* itself for both students and teachers (Wexler-Sherman, Gardner, & Feldman, 1988), and it leaves the responsibility for evaluation solely on the shoulders of teachers; students play a passive role (Johnston, 1987).

We have also made use of behaviorally stated instructional objectives for many years in lesson and activity plans; behavioral objectives are useful for short-term purposes in lesson planning and for measuring progress in the development of specific skills. While behavioral objectives can help us to determine if a lesson has been effective in some ways, they can serve only a small part in the overall assessment process.

If we consider the importance of assessing individual student progress in domains other than linguistic and logical-mathematical, neither examinations nor behavioral objectives will be totally adequate. A teacher may feel, for example, that interdisciplinary unit activities should foster cooperation and help promote interpersonal skills among students. To evaluate progress in these areas, direct observations of students will be needed; tests will not be effective in measuring those skills. Neither is testing very helpful in determining students' interests and attitudes or feelings about their own progress; realistically, examinations rarely invite students to participate in evaluating their own work. Instead, we have an option: ***authentic assessment.***

Authentic Assessment

Many teachers have traditionally collected representative examples of students' work in folders to use when conferring with parents. Collections of authentic materials, which represent the actual work produced by students in their day-to-day activities, are assembled by both students and teachers. Because students take part in selecting the samples, they are encouraged to become actively involved in the process of their own evaluation.

Assessment **portfolios** can be exceptionally useful evaluation tools because they indicate concretely what students are gaining from their work in school, and they provide a vehicle for reflection and interaction between students and their teachers. A portfolio also adds authentic evidence that can be combined with more objective and formal evaluation techniques, such as examinations.

A portfolio is referred to as an **authentic** assessment device because it includes actual examples of a student's work and surveys of his or her interests, feelings, and attitudes. It can often indicate growth in areas where examinations tend to be ineffective. When students are responsible for maintaining their own portfolios or parts of their portfolios, they can follow their own development. If they are asked to provide some notation for the materials they decide to include in their own portfolios, the process becomes even more reflective for them.

A portfolio prepared by the student—or student and teacher—can include many kinds of materials that are useful in the overall assessment process. Johnston (1992) explains that a student portfolio is analogous to an artist's portfolio because the student has the opportunity to include "work that she sees fit to display and talk about to others" (p. 129). The following list indicates some of the more common materials usually found in student portfolios:

- Examples of students' work and work in progress: creative and practical writing, experiments, creative work in the arts and music, photographs of projects completed or in progress
- Notes and memos
- Student observations and analyses of what was gained from instruction; what has been understood and not understood
- Teacher observations
- Surveys of feelings and attitudes
- Individual interest surveys
- Journals kept by students that include personal reflections and evaluations of their own work in the class
- Self-evaluations prepared by students
- Journals kept by teachers, reflecting on individual progress
- Teachers' anecdotal records
- Records of individual pupil/teacher conferences
- Formal and informal quizzes, tests, and examinations
- Recordings—audio- or videotapes—of oral readings, reports, or recitations

Selecting the materials for a portfolio needs to be a thoughtful process. Materials selected should provide for balance, with examples that represent both processes and products. Work samples need to include products that are in progress as well as those that have been completed (Pappas, Kiefer, & Levstik, 1995). It is also important to develop some criteria for students to use when choosing the samples they want to include, to decide how the materials will be evaluated and weighted in the overall assessment process, and to decide what part others, such as parents, may be required to play in evaluating a student's progress over time (Borich, 1996).

Preliminary research on the portfolio technique indicates that portfolios are having a positive effect on the improvement of instruction and an impact on the insight students have about their own academic strengths and weaknesses (O'Neill, 1993). For more information on authentic assessment and portfolio evaluation, readers are referred to the discussions and explanations in Charbonneau and Reider (1995), Darling-Hammond, Ancess, and Falk (1995), Ellis (1995), Lescher (1995), Viadero (1995), Wasserstein (1994), and Grosvenor (1993).

Examinations

As indicated earlier, most examinations are designed to measure verbal and logical-mathematical achievement; therefore, paper-and-pencil tests can be only a part of the total evaluation process. Nonetheless, examinations are still common evaluation tools in most schools, and most teachers continue to use them in their work. In interdisciplinary instruction, we need to determine if students have gained specific facts or concepts as a result of a unit of study. For many students, a comprehensive unit examination can be helpful in assessing the degree to which they have developed those concepts.

The preparation of an examination that will yield useful information about student achievement is never an easy task, primarily because a test can be an effective instrument only if it is both **valid** and **reliable.** The validity of a test depends on several factors. First, the test items included need to address only the objectives for which the test is designed. For example, if a teacher intends to prepare a test to determine if students have gained specific concepts from their unit on "The Middle East," then the test items—the questions—must all address those concepts. *Is the test actually evaluating what it is intended to evaluate?* is the main question in determining the validity of an examination.

Another factor that can have a considerable effect on the validity of a test is its **readability.** If a test is designed to assess students' conceptual knowledge from a unit of study and not, specifically, their ability to read the test, then the readability of the questions on the test must be at a level low enough for the students to read independently. Otherwise, the test may be measuring the students' reading ability as well as their mastery of concepts.

Test reliability is also a major concern. *Is the result of this examination a reliable estimate of what students have gained from their work?* is the important question in determining the reliability of any examination. A test cannot be reliable if it is not valid to begin with or if the directions for the test or any part of it are unclear to students. Directions should be clarified in advance to ensure that students understand them, and the directions should also be written on the test paper so that students can refer to them when necessary.

A test's reliability can also be seriously affected by both its length and the amount of time allotted for students to complete it. In general, a test will be likely to have greater reliability if it includes a larger sampling of students' knowledge by having enough test items and by allowing students enough time to complete those items. For example, with the exception of some essay examinations, a test having only a few test items will inadequately sample what students may have gained from their work. Of course, the length of a test needs to be reasonable for the amount of time that will be devoted to it, and most examinations should be prepared so that all students can complete them without the pressure of time constraints. Only speed and accuracy tests need to be restricted to severe time limits.

There are two general categories for the test items teachers prepare when writing examination questions: (1) ***supply*** items, where students need to provide the answers themselves, as in sentence completion, fill-ins, short answer, and essay items; and (2) ***objective*** items, where students are provided with choices from which to select their responses, as in true/false, multiple choice, and matching formats.

Certainly, special care is required when preparing questions for any test. By following several general guidelines for writing test items in the various formats, teachers can help to ensure that their questions are clear and that each test item addresses the objectives for which a test is specifically designed.

Nearly every educational psychology textbook and some generic methods texts include information on test item construction. Especially thorough are the test construction sections in books by Cangelosi (1990), Dembo (1988), Woolfolk (1987), Kourilsky and Quaranta (1987), Davis (1983), Guerin and Maier (1983), Lindemann and Merenda (1979), and Scannell and Tracy (1975). The following is a summary of test item construction suggestions with examples for each format, which can help to ensure higher validity and reliability of an examination.

Short answer or fill-in item suggestions:

Maintain uniformity in the length of blanks on a completion test to avoid suggesting the length of different words. Keep all blanks long enough for the longest word that will need to be written.

Include only one blank per test item to avoid the possibility that the test will be testing for closure or use of context clues in addition to its intended objective.

Examples

(Poor)   A _____ is used in a house to help prevent the _____ of the electrical _____.

(Better)   The overheating of electrical wiring in a house may be prevented if _____ breakers are installed.

Use one blank, even for names having two separate words, such as *Los Angeles* and *New York*. Two separate lines may suggest the correct answer.

Word the test item so that the blank appears either at or near the end of the statement. If the blank appears early in the sentence, students will need to rely heavily on closure and context clues to determine the meaning of the needed word. Unless the test is a test to determine the student's ability to use context clues, locate the blank near the end of the statement.

Examples

(Poor) _____ is the most important product in Brazil.

(Better) The most important product in Brazil is _____.

Include a word or phrase that indicates the category to which the answer must fit. For example, if a the statement calls for the name of a country, the student will know that unless a country is named, the answer cannot be correct. Giving a direct indication of the kind of information that must be included in the blank for a fill-in response helps to lessen ambiguity and the possibility of multiple correct answers.

Examples

(Poor) When did the English first arrive in North America?
_____

(Better) In what year did the English first arrive in North America?
_____

Avoid copying material directly from sources students have used for their information. The quoting of text material for an informal test not only condones plagiarism, but also encourages students to memorize the text instead of developing genuine comprehension of concepts.

Check all test items on a test to determine if one of the questions actually gives students an answer to another item.

Always use clear syntax and correct grammar and punctuation in writing any items.

Essay item suggestions:

Phrase questions so that they clearly indicate the task. Be precise about what and how much information is expected in the response.

When there are several essay items on a test, suggesting time allotments for each item may help students to budget their time.

In general, the practice of offering choices on essay examinations is not advisable. If each essay item is addressing an important objective, there is little reason to tell students that only "three of five" items need to be answered; any item that is not important should not appear on the exam. An exception to this rule can be made when the purpose of the test is to determine if students can write a well-developed essay; students may then be given a choice of topics.

Develop grading criteria before administering the test. Prepare an outline of what is expected for a complete answer to each essay question, and decide how to weigh the information required in each essay response before beginning the grading process.

Use a consistent scoring method: either a rating scale or holistic scoring. Establish a policy for handling other factors, such as any irrelevant information students include, and the mechanics of spelling, handwriting, punctuation, grammar, and syntax.

It is often a good idea to read all students' responses to one essay question before reading others; i.e., read all student responses to the first essay question, then continue to read all responses to the second, etc. Comparing all responses to the same essay question may help to maintain a more even scoring of the responses, especially when using a holistic grading method.

Examples

(Poor)	Discuss what you have learned about the British Parliament and the United States Congress.
(Better)	Describe two major differences and one similarity between the British Parliament and the United States Congress.

True/false item suggestions:

Keep the wording succinct and clear.

Avoid broad, general statements and words such as *always, never, all, may seldom, usually,* etc.

Use negatives sparingly at all grade levels, and always draw attention to the negative word with an underline, italics, or bold type. Avoid negatives altogether in examinations for children in the primary grades because very young children have considerable difficulty with reversals in thought.

Avoid ambiguity in the statement. A true/false item should be unequivocally true or false.

Keep the items as uniform in length as possible.

Nearly balance the numbers of true and false items. When there is an overbalance of either, students may be led to believe they must have answered some questions incorrectly.

Examples

(Poor)	__ Birds eat more than mammals.
	__ Martha and George Washington had two children.
(Better)	__ Considering body weight, birds eat more than mammals.
	__ Martha and George Washington raised two children.

Multiple-choice item suggestions:

A multiple-choice test item is composed of two parts: a **stem** and several **answer choices.** The stem should present enough information so that the answer choices can be relatively short. Having to read lengthy choices after reading the stem may be testing students' short-term memory; unless this is the purpose of the test, this memory factor may interfere with the item's validity.

Use negatives sparingly, and highlight them if they are used. Avoid negatives in tests for children in the primary grades.

Determiners, such as *all*, *some*, *often*, *usually*, etc., should be avoided.

Use special alternatives, such as *all of the above* and *none of the above*, sparingly.

Try to keep the answer choices similar in length to avoid suggesting that any particular answer is the correct one.

Make sure that all of the answer choices are somewhat feasible while ensuring that there is only one correct answer.

Ensure that all answer choices are grammatically consistent with the stem of the item.

Poor Example

An example of:

A. an animal that is a mollusk is a whale.

B. an animal that is a mollusk is a clam.

C. an animal that is a mollusk is a crab.

D. an animal that is a mollusk is a lobster.

Better Example

An example of a mollusk is a:

A. whale.

B. clam.

C. crab.

D. lobster.

Matching item suggestions:

Each matching item is composed of a set of **premises** and **response choices** listed in two columns. Keep each matching set relatively short because requiring students to search through too many choices for an answer may test their short-term memory as well as their knowledge of the material for which the test is intended, thus lowering the test's validity. Try to limit any matching set to seven or fewer premises. Prepare a new and separate set if more items need to be tested.

The material being tested in a single matching set should be as homogeneous as possible. For example, if testing about simple machines, avoid other topics.

Include as much material in the premises as needed, but keep the length of response choices relatively short to avoid testing short-term memory instead of content.

Include one or two extra response choices to avoid the certainty that a student who has one answer wrong will have another wrong.

Place the entire matching set on one page.

Poor Example

	Column A	Column B
_____	1. Thermometer	A. An instrument that measures humidity
_____	2. Barometer	B. An instrument that measures rainfall
_____	3. Wind vane	C. An instrument that measures wind direction
_____	4. Rain gauge	D. An instrument that measures temperature
_____	5. Hygrometer	

Better Example

	Column A	Column B
_____	1. An instrument that measures wind direction	A. Thermometer
_____	2. An instrument that measures temperature	B. Barometer
_____	3. An instrument that measures humidity	C. Wind vane
_____	4. An instrument that measures rainfall	D. Humidifier
_____	5. An instrument that measures air pressure	E. Hygrometer
		F. Telemeter
		G. Rain gauge

Planning Learning Centers

It is often possible to use other teaching strategies, such as learning centers, with interdisciplinary units. Learning centers have been popular with teachers for many years. Including them in interdisciplinary studies can provide students with extra skills practice, more independent work on tasks involving one or more discipline, additional creative writing activities, and opportunities for more creative work with art media.

There are several types of learning centers. Simple, interactive centers can be constructed using a bulletin board with pockets for written directions for a variety of tasks or problem-solving activities the students can select to work on individually. Learning centers can be displayed on an empty shelf or other flat surface in the classroom. In more elaborate centers, the materials and activities to be used are arranged on a table or group of tables in a designated area. Space may be provided for students to work at the center, or they can be directed to take the activities from the center to their seats or another part of the room. The specific form a learning center takes always depends on both its purpose and the classroom space available to set it up.

Developing a learning center requires a considerable amount of planning and preparation. To help ensure that a learning center will be effective in developing the learnings for which it is intended, several important procedures need to be followed:

1. First, decide the purpose or purposes the center will serve.

2. Select a central theme for the center. *(When used with an interdisciplinary unit, the theme is either the unit theme or one that is related to the unit.)*

3. Determine the specific activities to be included in the learning center. These can include a variety of interdisciplinary tasks, problems to be solved, construction activities, science experiments, readings, research, writing, or other activities that seem appropriate for the children who will use the center.

4. Prepare *task cards.* Task cards give specific directions the children will need to complete each activity included in the center. An example of a task card shown in Figure 4.3 has directions for a group of fourth-grade children who are studying an interdisciplinary unit on deserts in the United States. (This theme is used in Chapter 6 to develop a research-oriented thematic unit for children in an intermediate grade).

FIGURE 4.3
Sample task card for
a desert collage

> **Desert Collage**
>
> In this activity, you will make a collage to show what you have learned from watching a filmstrip on the Mohave Desert.
>
> *Directions:*
>
> 1. Use the filmstrip projector in the learning center to watch the filmstrip, "The Mohave Desert."
>
> 2. Take a sheet of construction paper from the supply section in the learning center. Write your name on the back of the paper. Paste, glue, tape, and other supplies for your work are kept in our regular supply closet. Take paint and paint brushes if you would like to use them.
>
> 3. Use materials from our scrap box to prepare a collage that shows something specific you have learned from the filmstrip.
>
> 4. Be prepared to describe your collage during one of our regular "forums" at the end of each day this week.

5. Assemble the equipment and materials needed for the activities. Art supplies, science equipment, textbooks and trade books, charts, picture collections, duplicated worksheets, diagrams, and other items the children will need should be supplied in or near the center.

6. Provide space and equipment for students to use when interacting with any audiovisual materials that are to be included in the center: computer programs, tape recordings, filmstrips, and videotapes.

7. Prepare a schedule for use of the center—a sign-up sheet or teacher-prepared list—to ensure that all the children have an opportunity to use the center over a period of time.

8. Develop a record-keeping device for assessing students' use of the center activities or to monitor their participation. A simple checklist of students' names and activities is usually adequate for this purpose. See Figure 4.4 for a sample checklist.

9. Designate a place for the students to leave their completed work.

10. Decide how to introduce the learning center to the class. Most students thoroughly enjoy using learning centers, and they may become anxious to begin as soon as they see it appear in the classroom. A thorough introduction can set routines and guidelines for using the center in advance that will help to deter problems that can arise from misuse of learning center activities or materials. A set of directions should be prepared for children to read before they work with any of the learning center activities. An example of a directions poster is shown in Figure 4.5.

FIGURE 4.4
Sample checklist for a learning center

Check (x) the activities you have completed.	Learning Center Activities									
Name	1	2	3	4	5	6	7	8	9	10
Kim	X			X	X		X			
Kevin	X	X	X							
Shannon					X	X				X
Allison	X						X			
Nina		X	X	X	X					
Salvatore	X					X		X		X
Jennifer	X		X	X					X	
John						X	X		X	
Maria		X	X			X				
Carmen				X	X			X		X
Shawna								X	X	X
Jim		X	X							

FIGURE 4.5
Example of a directions poster

Using the Desert Learning Center

1. Before you begin to work in the learning center, look at all the activities to learn the different choices you will have.

2. Select one activity to begin, and follow the directions carefully on the task card included with that activity.

3. If the task requires another person to participate, you can choose someone to work with you.

4. When you finish an activity, find your name on the record sheet, and make a check in the box next to the activity you have completed.

5. Remember to replace all materials and to keep the learning center neat and orderly for others to use.

Clearly, interdisciplinary units do not prevent teachers from using other valuable teaching strategies. Learning centers are especially effective for providing students with opportunities to work independently on tasks related to their units, and they can be used at all grade levels. This brief overview of learning centers will not be adequate for teachers who are not already familiar with the technique. For a current, comprehensive discussion of learning centers, readers are referred to an excellent explanation by Fredericks and Cheesebrough (1993, pp. 186–93). Also, the earlier handbooks by Kaplan et al. (1980) and Fisk and Lindgren (1974) offer teachers two of the more thorough presentations on this topic. A manual that is helpful for teachers who want to develop a learning center for a single discipline is the one prepared by Poppe and Van Matre (1985).

This chapter has presented a general overview of some important considerations and strategies for teachers who are beginning to plan for interdisciplinary instruction. The next two chapters will elaborate on the planning processes for two types of interdisciplinary units — thematic and research-oriented thematic unit plans.

References

Bloom, B. S. (1956). *Taxonomy of educational goals, by a committee of college and university examiners.* New York: Longmans, Green.

Borich, G. D. (1996). *Effective teaching methods* (3rd ed.). Upper Saddle River, NJ: Merrill/Prentice Hall.

Bruner, J. (1963). *The process of education.* New York: Vintage.

Cangelosi, J. S. (1990). *Designing tests for evaluating student achievement.* New York: Longman.

Charbonneau, M. P., & Reider, B. E. (1995). *The integrated elementary classroom: A developmental model of education for the 21st century.* Needham Heights, MA: Allyn & Bacon.

Darling-Hammond, L. (1994). Setting standards for students: The case for authentic assessment. *The Educational Forum, 59*(1), 14–21.

Darling-Hammond, L., Ancess, J., & Falk, B. (1995). *Authentic assessment in action: Studies of schools and students at work.* New York: Teachers College Press.

Davies, I. K. (1976). *Objectives in curriculum design.* London: McGraw-Hill.

Davis, G. A. (1983). *Educational psychology: Theory and practice.* Reading, MA: Addison-Wesley.

Dembo, M. H. (1988). *Applying educational psychology in the classroom* (3rd ed.). New York: Longman.

Dick, W., & Carey, L. (1978). *The systematic design of instruction.* Glenview, IL: Scott, Foresman.

Ellis, A. K. (1995). *Teaching and learning elementary social studies* (5th ed.). Needham Heights, MA: Allyn & Bacon.

Engel, B. S. (1994). Portfolio assessment and the new paradigm: New instruments and new places. *The Educational Forum, 59*(1), 22–27.

Fisk, L., & Lindgren, H. (1974). *Learning centers.* Glen Ridge, NJ: Exceptional Press.

Fredericks, A., & Cheesebrough, D. (1993). *Science for all children: Elementary school methods.* New York: Harper Collins.

Gronlund, N. E. (1985). *Stating objectives for classroom instruction* (3rd ed.). New York: Macmillan.

Grosvenor, L. (1993). *Student portfolios.* Washington, DC: National Education Association.

Guerin, G. R., & Maier, A. S. (1983). *Informal assessment in education.* Palo Alto, CA: Mayfield.

Jacobs, H. (Ed.). (1989). *Interdisciplinary curriculum: Design and implementation.* Alexandria, VA: Association for Supervision and Curriculum Development.

Johnston, P. (1987). Teachers as evaluation experts. *The Reading Teacher, 40,* 744–48.

Johnston, P. H. (1992). *Constructive evaluation of literate activity.* White Plains, NY: Longman.

Kaplan, S. N., Kaplan, J. B., Madsen, S. K., & Gould, B. T. (1980). *Change for children: Ideas and activities for individualizing learning.* Glenview, IL: Scott, Foresman.

Kibler, R. J., Cegala, D. J., Barker, L. L., & Miles, D. T. (1974). *Objectives for instruction and evaluation* (2nd ed.). Boston: Allyn & Bacon.

Kourilsky, M., & Quaranta, L. (1987). *Effective teaching: Principles and Practice.* Glenview, IL: Scott, Foresman.

Lescher, M. L. (1995). *Portfolios: Assessing learning in the primary grades.* Washington, DC: National Education Association.

Lindemann, R. H., & Merenda, P. F. (1979). *Educational measurement* (2nd ed.). Glenview, IL: Scott, Foresman.

Mager, R. (1984). *Preparing instructional objectives* (Rev. 2nd ed.). Belmont, CA: Lake Management & Training.

O'Neill, J. (1993, September). The promise of portfolios. *Update, 35*(7), 1–5.

Pappas, C. C., Kiefer, B. Z., & Levstik, L. S. (1995). *An integrated language perspective in the elementary school.* White Plains, NY: Longman.

Poppe, C. A., & Van Matre, N. A. (1985). *Science learning centers for primary grades.* West Nyack, NY: Center for Applied Research in Education.

Ravich, D. (1988). Tot sociology. *American Educator, 12*(3), 38–9.

Scannell, D. P., & Tracy, D. B. (1975). *Testing and measurement in the classroom.* Boston: Houghton Mifflin.

Viadero, D. (1995, April 5). Even as popularity soars, portfolios encounter roadblocks. *Education Week,* pp. 8–9.

Wasserstein, P. (1994, Fall). To do or not to do portfolios: That is the question. *Kappa Delta Pi Record, 31*(1), 12–15.

Wexler-Sherman, C., Gardner, H., & Feldman, D. H. (1988). A pluralistic view of early assessment: The project spectrum approach. *Theory Into Practice, 27,* 77–83.

Woolfolk, A. E. (1987). *Educational psychology* (3rd ed.). Upper Saddle River, NJ: Prentice Hall.

Suggested Readings

The readings listed below offer additional background material for the teaching strategies discussed in this chapter, including preparation of instructional objectives, questioning techniques, Bloom's Taxonomy, evaluation, and the planning of learning centers.

Clark, B. (1986). *Optimizing learning: The integrative education model in the classroom.* Upper Saddle River, NJ: Merrill/Prentice Hall.

Crain, A. A. (1993). *Teaching science through discovery* (7th ed.). New York: Merrill/Macmillan.

Katz, L., & Chard, S. C. (1989). *Engaging children's minds: The project approach.* Norwood, NJ: Ablex Publishing.

McNeil, J. D., & Wiles, J. (1990). *The essentials of teaching: Decisions, plans, methods.* New York: Macmillan.

Peterson, R., Bowyer, J., Butts, D., & Bybee, R. (1984). *Science and society: A source book for elementary and junior high school teachers.* Upper Saddle River, NJ: Merrill/Prentice Hall.

White, A. M. (Ed.). (1981). *Interdisciplinary teaching.* San Francisco: Jossey–Bass.

Wilen, W. W. (Ed.). (1987). *Questions, questioning techniques, and effective teaching.* Washington, DC: National Education Association.

5

Designing Thematic Units

This chapter describes and illustrates an eight-step procedure for planning thematic units for students at all grade levels. Examples are provided for each step in the procedure. The chapter includes:

- *An outline for a complete thematic unit plan.*
- *A description of eight steps in the planning process, along with explanations and examples at each step in designing a thematic unit on "Spring" for children in the second grade.*
- *A complete sample unit plan on "Spring."*

Thematic Unit Plan Outline

The eight-step procedure explained and illustrated in this chapter will provide the information needed to design a thematic unit plan. Most unit plan formats include objectives, procedures to be followed, important materials needed for the unit, and evaluation techniques to be used for assessment. Figure 5.1 shows an outline for a thematic unit plan and the headings for each of its major sections.

FIGURE 5.1
A thematic unit plan outline

Theme:

Estimated Length:

Title:

Level:

General Objectives:

Diagram of the Plan:

Introductory Lesson Plan:

    Topic:

    Level:

    General Objective:

    Time:

    Behavioral Objective:

    Procedure:

    Materials:

Descriptions of Lessons and Activities:

Evaluation Techniques:

Materials:

This outline can be used to design thematic unit plans for students at all grade levels: primary, intermediate, and middle school. The planning task and specific kinds of information to be included under each heading in the unit plan outline are as follows:

Theme
State the theme of the unit.

Estimated Length
Estimate the amount of time that will be needed to teach the unit.

Title
List title suggestions and possible ways to involve students in deciding on a title for their unit.

Level
State the grade or grades for which the unit is intended. Although only the grade level needs to appear here, the students' background and readiness for the unit, their social and developmental characteristics, and their academic abilities will need to be considered when making decisions about the appropriateness of any unit theme.

General Objectives
Statements in this section suggest the overall purposes for which the unit is designed. General objectives reveal the content, important concepts the unit will aim to develop, its affective goals, and any learning processes the teacher hopes to promote throughout the study.

Diagram of the Plan
Design a web that suggests the possible lessons, interdisciplinary activities, and skills to be taught during the unit. Show ways those ideas relate to the various disciplines and to one another. The web should indicate that provisions have been made for students' differing cognitive strengths and styles of learning. An optional introduction can be written to accompany the web to provide other teachers with a rationale for teaching the unit, to show the major concepts it is intended to develop, and to indicate that the unit is interdisciplinary.

Introductory Lesson Plan
Using the lesson plan outline that follows, plan the first lesson for the unit. This lesson will be used to introduce the unit to the students. The same outline can also be used for other lessons and unit activities, or other lesson planning formats can be substituted, such as those outlined by Roberts and Kellough (1996), Ellis (1995), or Kauchak and Eggen (1993); the MI (multiple intelligences) lesson plan outlined by Armstrong (1994); or the "new style" lesson plan recommended by McNeil and Wiles (1990).

Topic: State the unit theme and main topic of the lesson.

Level: State the age level(s) or grade(s) for which the lesson is designed.

General Objectives: State one or more general objectives for the lesson.

Time: Estimate the amount of time that will be needed for the lesson or activity.

Behavioral Objectives: State the specific objective(s) for the lesson.

Procedure: Write a paragraph or a sequential list of steps detailing the procedure for the lesson. Include anticipated student responses when feasible.

Materials: List the essential materials needed for the lesson.

Descriptions of Lessons and Activities

This section of the unit plan expands on the idea suggestions found in the web by adding details that could not be included in the web itself (in order to keep it from becoming overcrowded). In this section, write a complete description for each lesson or activity idea listed in the diagram. Follow each description with a statement to explain the purpose(s) for including it in the unit.

Evaluation Techniques

Although the behavioral objectives for lessons and activities will help to assess their effectiveness, other, more comprehensive measures are often used. List those other evaluation techniques, such as portfolio assessment and examinations to be used in the overall unit evaluation.

Materials

List major materials needed for the unit. Titles of films, video programs, filmstrips, computer software, and other media can be included for reference. Specific titles, however, may become outdated, and each time the unit is taught, new materials may become available. Therefore, when the unit is first being planned, a simple list indicating the *types* of texts, trade books, and other materials may suffice until the unit is under way.

An Eight-Step Procedure for Developing a Thematic Unit Plan

Thematic units are appropriate for students at all elementary and middle school grade levels. Primary grade teachers find thematic units especially well suited to the developmental characteristics and academic abilities of their young children. Teachers in the intermediate grades and middle school can teach thematic units, or they can use a modification of the thematic design that involves considerably more reading-related research activities, a **research-oriented thematic unit.** (The design of a research-oriented thematic unit plan and the steps involved in developing it are explained and illustrated in Chapter 6.)

In order to develop material needed for a complete thematic unit plan, an eight-step procedure will be outlined, explained, and illustrated with examples. The intent here is to present a planning procedure for preservice and inservice teachers who are learning to design interdisciplinary thematic units for the *first* time. The process outlined in this chapter will develop an *initial* unit plan only, a plan that will need to be modified and updated each time it is taught to a new group of students.

It is recommended that those who have not previously studied interdisciplinary unit planning follow each step in the sequence outlined in this chapter. Later, once the eight-step process is mastered, it can easily be modified to suit one's personal teaching style and planning needs. The sequence presented here conforms closely to conventional practice with one exception: the step for writing formal (behavioral) objectives is placed after designing the procedure for lessons and activities.

Traditionally, teachers have been taught to *begin* planning by stating their objectives and then to plan a procedure to meet those objectives. However, it is possible that if they begin the planning process with formal, written objective statements, especially with behavioral statements, the creativity they might be able to bring to the planning process will be inhibited. In fact, the entire planning process may become regimented by the wording in the objectives.

Although specific objective statements need not be written before planning a procedure, it is nevertheless essential to have some general purposes in mind for a lesson or activity before beginning to plan a procedure. Overall purposes may include the development of concepts, providing students with opportunities to practice the learning processes, and helping them to gain further insights in the different ways of knowing associated with the various academic disciplines.

As long as general purposes are considered first, writing formal, behaviorally stated objectives can be delayed until after thinking creatively about the procedure. Readers will therefore find in the eight-step procedure that writing both the general unit objectives and the behavioral objective for the initial lesson plan appear later in the planning process than is conventional practice. Teachers who feel that preparing behavioral objectives should precede any other planning step should do so, but realize that objective statements should not dictate the procedure for the lesson.

Once the teacher has selected a theme and has general purposes or informal objectives in mind, the eight-step process can begin. Several of the eight steps listed here can be completed quickly; two will require more time:

1. Consider the students' developmental abilities, cognitive strengths and limitations, learning and working styles, knowledge, and experiential background for the theme to be studied.

2. Brainstorm for possible procedures: lessons and activities that will address the different disciplines and students' *multiple intelligences*. Prepare a graphic web, showing the basic ideas for teaching skills and other lessons, field trips, science inquiries and experiments, research, and related activities.

3. Prepare a complete plan for the initial lesson or activity that will be used to introduce the unit.

4. Write brief descriptions of other lessons and activities. (The descriptions substitute, temporarily, for complete plans that will need to be developed later if the ideas are actually used once the unit begins.)

5. List general objectives for the entire unit.

6. List tentative evaluation methods and techniques.

7. List essential materials.

8. Decide the unit title, or develop a method of involving the students in selecting a title.

If a unit plan is to be shared later with other teachers, an **introduction,** a one-paragraph statement, can be inserted after the unit plan diagram—the web—to explain the purpose of the unit and to summarize the interdisciplinary procedures suggested in the web design.

Each of the eight steps to be followed when preparing a thematic unit plan is explained next along with several examples at each of those steps. For illustrative purposes, material for a primary-level unit plan on the theme, "Spring," will be generated as the steps are explained. The reason for selecting this particular theme is that it offers children a number of opportunities to have direct experiences related to the concept and the processes of "change," an important concept in both the social studies and science curriculums. At each step in the eight-step procedure, only a few examples from the "Spring" unit will be shown; a complete sample unit plan for the "Spring" theme can be found at the end of this chapter.

Step One: Considering Children's Developmental Abilities and Background for the Theme

This step may well be the most important one in the entire planning process. Whenever they plan, successful teachers attend to the critical match between the cognitive abilities of children in their classes and the new facts, concepts, and generalizations to be developed in their units. Estimating the thinking and reasoning levels of children in advance of teaching helps to minimize the chance that children will meet with frustration.

Contrary to Piaget's estimate that children in the primary grades are still primarily egocentric and that their thinking patterns are totally preoperational, we have evidence from post-Piagetian research that Piaget may have underestimated the cognitive abilities of these young children. Even before the second or early third grade, many children may have developed more sophisticated thinking and reasoning skills, especially if they have been provided with adequate instruction and have had opportunities to interact with adults and competent peers.

It is still essential for children in the primary grades to have direct, hands-on experiences. Those concrete experiences can easily be brought to primary-level thematic units. Children can conduct their own inquiries and experiments in science and use concrete materials to develop concepts in mathematics. They develop their spatial abilities by working with art media and producing art to show some of the concepts they are gaining. Typical art activities include painting murals and working with art projects and media, such as papier-mâché, playdough, and clay, to form artifacts, dioramas, and other constructions.

Teachers can also provide concrete experiences for young children by organizing field trips, especially to places where they are permitted not only to observe but also to interact physically with real objects. Music is a pathway to learning for many children, and teachers can offer opportunities to learn about the world through singing, experimenting with simple musical instruments, and listening to recordings. The only techniques that are not defendable, from a developmental point of view, include substituting teacher demonstrations and lectures and whole class, oral reading from textbooks in place of concrete learning experiences.

Development in the affective and psychomotor domains should also be considered. Knowledge of children's individual feelings, attitudes, and temperaments and the ways they interact with one another is valuable when planning unit activities. Information about the children's motor coordination and their health and physical development is also critical, particularly when planning outdoor activities or field trips or when planning to prepare food.

It is equally important to learn as much as possible about the children's experiential and knowledge background for the theme to be studied. New information in the unit can be assimilated only if it builds on the students' existing knowledge base; in order to avoid frustration and failure, students must have a foundation for any new material they are expected to assimilate.

Of course, knowing students' developmental and academic abilities is always more difficult during the early months of a school year than it will be later on after having worked with them for several months. Nevertheless, this step cannot be avoided whenever a new unit is being planned, and in the early months, teachers should estimate as well as they can students' readiness for the units they plan to teach.

The following is a description of the second-grade class for which the interdisciplinary unit on "Spring" will be designed in this chapter. Note that in the description, there is information about the children's previous study and background for the new unit. Their thinking, academic abilities, social characteristics, special needs, and talents are also outlined.

The children in this heterogeneous group of second graders are mainly preoperational in their thinking and reasoning abilities; they will need hands-on experiences whenever possible to help them develop concepts in their unit on "Spring." Some of the children will be capable of reading for information; however, most children in the group have not yet developed independent reading levels adequate for many of the books and other resources available on this topic. Socially, the children get along well with one another, although there are occasional conflicts and minor behavioral problems. Four children have special needs: one child is physically handicapped, and one has been diagnosed with a specific learning disability; one child has a special talent for mathematics and another for art. Other children have strength in music. The class has completed a unit on the concept "neighborhood." That unit focused on learning about the children's local neighborhood, and their most recent thematic unit, "Our School," expanded their knowledge of concepts related to the neighborhood unit. It is early spring in an elementary school in the northeast, and many children have indicated their interest in the weather changes they have noticed.

FIGURE 5.2
An "idea" web design

Step Two: Brainstorming for Possible Procedures and Preparing a Graphic Design or Web of the Procedures

Teachers will recognize this step as another critical one in planning for any instruction. Because the intent is to develop *interdisciplinary* plans, designing a web showing anticipated disciplines and activities can help to ensure interdisciplinarity of the plan. There are a number of ways the design can be charted. One approach is to begin with the theme at the center of the diagram, then list all brainstormed ideas related to the theme radiating out from the center, as shown in Figure 5.2. Pappas, Kiefer, and Levstik (1995) and Stephens (1974) use variations of this arrangement for their thematic webs.

If this model is used, it is possible that some important disciplines or study areas will be overlooked. In order to avoid that possibility, once the theme is centered in the web, names of the major disciplines can be pictured surrounding the theme. The design can then be completed with brief statements about the central idea of each brainstormed idea: the activities and lessons. See Figure 5.3 for a web showing both disciplines and planning ideas radiating from the central theme.

FIGURE 5.3
A thematic unit planning
web design

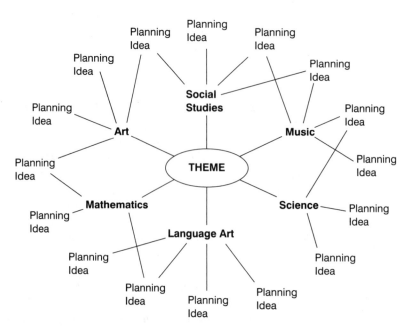

Charbonneau and Reider (1995) and Jacobs (1989) show examples similar to this particular model. All of the models accomplish the major purpose of the web: to chart possibilities for an interdisciplinary plan. After some experience with any design, most planners will find that each design offers some unique advantages and that the designs can easily be modified to suit personal preferences.

Before beginning to brainstorm, teachers should prepare several lists: a list of ***disciplines,*** a list of interdisciplinary ***general areas of concern,*** and a list of teaching ***strategies and techniques***. These lists will not only assist the brainstorming process but will also help to ensure that the unit is interdisciplinary and comprehensive. Three example lists are shown in Figure 5.4.

Some teachers may question including such abstract areas as political science, global issues, and future studies for children in the primary grades. However, it is important to consider that children have a natural curiosity about people in other parts of the world, and today, they often express concern for environmental problems. Although children may have some difficulty comprehending the global issues they hear about, teachers can supply explanations and offer to discuss those issues using terms the children can understand. Those explanations may help to allay the fears that young children sometimes develop about world problems.

In the primary grades, children also enjoy thinking about both the past and the future. All of our history is in the past, sometimes making it a difficult subject for

Disciplines	General Areas of Concern	Media, Strategies, and Techniques
history	multiculturalism	computer technology
geography	values clarification	software
economics	ecology	Internet
mathematics	human behavior	multimedia
psychology	human rights	films
sociology	consumerism	filmstrips
anthropology	career education	video programs
science	civics	audio recordings
language arts	citizenship	experiments
listening	health	demonstrations
speaking	family living	skills lessons
reading	substance abuse	field trips
writing	global studies	group discussions
political science	space exploration	interviews/surveys
visual arts	future studies	research
performing arts	current events	reports
music	different working or	art projects
drama	learning styles	murals
dance		constructions
		charts and graphs
		time lines

FIGURE 5.4
A list of disciplines, general areas of concern, and teaching strategies and techniques

the very young to fully comprehend. Nevertheless, early childhood teachers certainly can include aspects of history in their thematic units. Today, we know that by selecting a variety of materials—not only textbooks—and by providing opportunities for children to use a variety of media and individual working styles, we can help young children to master concepts once thought to be beyond their understanding.

In the primary grades, children can usually relate better to historical events and concepts when they are discussed using terms such as "long ago" and "a long time before we were born." These are terms the children can relate to personally and that have special meaning for them.

The concept *future* is also problematic for young minds. Still, children are naturally interested in what the future will be like for them; they can and should be encouraged to think about it. Both the past and future become more meaningful when children use learning techniques, such as **time lines,** to plot historical events. Time lines can easily include each child's birth date to use as a meaningful personal reference point for the historical events they study.

Some disciplines and interdisciplinary areas tend to overlap or include very similar material. For example, human relations and conduct are components of both psychology and sociology. Human relations and values clarification issues are both included in multicultural studies. Many teachers may feel that other important categories or items need to be added to the lists in Figure 5.4. The lists can always be modified to meet individual teachers' purposes and special concerns.

While brainstorming, a diagram or web should be sketched in a graphic form to record the ideas that are generated. As explained earlier, the diagram is a simple drawing showing the disciplines along with ideas for lessons and activities that will potentially become part of the unit work. The diagram shows at a glance what is possible to include in the unit; lines can also be drawn to indicate ways the various disciplines, lessons, and activities relate to one another. The design will simply serve as a reminder of the brainstormed ideas so that, later on, complete lesson and activity plans can be written for the ideas that are actually used when the unit is taught.

When the web is completed, it will also suggest how long the unit will take to complete; the web is also useful in making decisions about how to sequence lessons and activities after the unit has been introduced to the children. A thematic unit may vary in length from only a few days in primary classes to four to six weeks or more in the intermediate grades and middle school.

The design in Figure 5.5 shows a few ideas the teacher has charted as the brainstorming step begins in planning a hypothetical second grade unit on the theme "Spring."

The teacher is just beginning to plan, so only a few activities are listed in the web at this point. The main theme is centered with several disciplines around it. So far, the teacher plans to take the children on a walking field trip in the local neighborhood to look for signs of spring. The children will use their observational skills to search for the signs they already know, and their teacher will encourage them to look for others they have not yet observed. The children will record their observations by drawing individual pictures, some of which will later be transferred to a mural. The purpose of the mural will be to help the children summarize the signs of spring they have observed while on their walk. Stories about spring will be read to the children, and

FIGURE 5.5
Initial stage in developing
the design for a thematic
unit on "Spring"

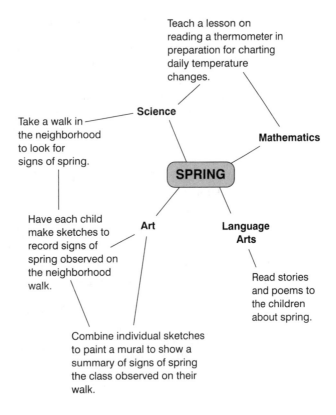

Teach a lesson on
reading a thermometer in
preparation for charting
daily temperature
changes.

Take a walk in
the neighborhood
to look for
signs of spring.

Science

Mathematics

SPRING

Have each child
make sketches to
record signs of
spring observed on
the neighborhood
walk.

Art

**Language
Arts**

Read stories
and poems to
the children
about spring.

Combine individual sketches
to paint a mural to show a
summary of signs of spring
the class observed on their
walk.

there will be a lesson on reading a thermometer. This lesson is in preparation for recording daily temperature changes throughout the unit.

Several academic disciplines—or domains—have been considered at this point in the unit's development: drawings of observations (spatial), a planning discussion in preparation for the field trip (linguistic), learning to read a thermometer (logical-mathematical), and working together on a mural (interpersonal).

Only the teacher's basic idea for each lesson or activity appears in the diagram, just enough information to use as a reminder if the idea is actually used. The brainstorming step and construction of the web help to set parameters for the unit and provide an overview of its development. As the "Spring" web continues to grow with further brainstorming, more ideas are charted, and lines are added to indicate some of the connections among the disciplines, lessons, and activities.

As indicated in Figure 5.6, additions to the original diagram indicate that the children will be keeping a record and preparing a graph of daily temperature readings. Additions to the original design also show that the children will listen to musical selections having spring as a theme; the same musical selections will also be used for a movement activity. These activities address two other cognitive areas or intelligences. In social studies, there will be lessons about any spring holidays that occur while the children are involved in the unit. (Additional ideas are included in the web for the complete "Spring" unit plan at the end of this chapter.)

Step Three: Planning the Initial Lesson for the Unit

The design of the first lesson or activity is a key factor in determining how successful a unit will be. Before beginning to plan the lesson, the teacher will consider the children's academic skill levels and developmental characteristics as well as the social makeup of the class. The initial lesson informs the children of the unit theme and attempts to engage their interest in the new study. General principles of teaching and learning can help to guide the lesson design. Three especially important principles for this unit follow:

- In order to be adapted, new information must build upon children's present knowledge base.

- Children will need to *construct* their own knowledge, personally, by using their different cognitive strengths, through direct experiences whenever feasible and through opportunities to interact with adults and peers.

- Motivation will be stronger if unit activities and lessons capitalize on the children's interests, working styles, and learning styles.

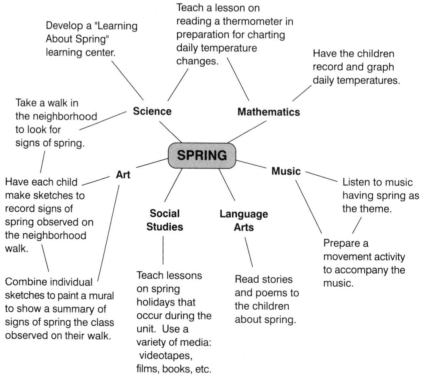

FIGURE 5.6
Additions to the initial design for a thematic unit on "Spring"

An idea for the first lesson or activity has been selected from the "Spring" web. The teacher has chosen an idea that appears likely to motivate and engage children's interest. (If none of the ideas in the web had seemed to be suitable, the teacher would have generated a new one specifically to introduce the unit.) The suggestion for a walk through the neighborhood to look for signs of spring was selected here for the first activity—or introductory lesson—in the "Spring" unit.

The field trip activity will take more than one class session; the introductory session or lesson will serve only to introduce the theme of the new unit and prepare the children for their trip. In the initial lesson, the teacher has decided to elicit from the children several signs of spring, which they will then keep in mind and look for during the field trip. When they actually take their walk, on another day, the children will also be encouraged to observe carefully and search for other signs they have not thought of in the preparatory session.

In the unit plan, the first lesson can be described in paragraph form, or it can be written as a sequence of numbered, procedural steps, much as it would in a conventional lesson plan. Two essential parts of the first lesson will be explained and illustrated: the *procedure* and the *behavioral objective*. (The lesson plan appears in its complete form at the end of the chapter.) The procedure for the introductory lesson in the "Spring" unit includes 11 steps; the first 7 steps are given to illustrate how the sequence looks as the teacher begins planning the lesson. Note that, in parentheses, the teacher has included some anticipated student responses to the questions they will be asked during the lesson.

Procedure:

1. Select a day for the field trip in advance, and secure the necessary permissions. Invite two adults from the list of parent volunteers to assist with supervision while on the walk. (The field trip will be taken after this introductory lesson, which is only preparing the children for their walk.)

2. The first lesson will begin with a class meeting in the early afternoon during the time regularly devoted to unit studies.

3. Begin the lesson by reminding the children that they have studied their neighborhood this year and that their last unit was "Our School." Ask the children to recall some activities from that unit. (*Children will probably say they remember drawing a map of the school, and visiting and interviewing several people who work in the school: the nurse, the school principal, and a custodian. They will also remember learning about the work the people do, that they actually saw where the people do their work, and that they were given a chance to see some materials the people use for their jobs. The children may also recall drawing and labeling pictures of school helpers.*)

4. Ask the children if they have noticed that the school custodians are beginning to do some work they have not been able to do all winter. (*The children may have noticed that the school custodians are working outside on the grounds.*)

5. Ask the children if they can think of any reasons why work is beginning outside at this time of year. *(Children will probably say that it is because the grass is growing and that it is warmer. They may also say it is now spring.)*

6. Tell the children that they will be studying this new season and that "spring" is the theme of their new unit.

7. Ask the children what they already know about the spring season. Write their responses on the board. A concept web will be used to record what the children say. (See Figure 5.7 for a web showing the children's initial concepts of spring.) *(Responses may include that it is a special time of the year, a time when the weather gets warmer and they no longer have to wear heavy clothing. They may say the grass and some flowers begin to grow in spring and that the trees have buds. Some may remember that there are some important holidays during the spring season.)*

The preceding list gives only part of the procedure for the lesson. Four steps are added in the complete procedure for the introductory lesson included in the "Spring" unit plan at the end of this chapter.

In step three, at the beginning of the plan, the teacher helps the children make a connection between what they have recently studied (their own school and the people who work in it) and their new unit on the season of spring. The children are asked to recall their interviews with people who work in the school and then to think why the school custodians are beginning to work outside on the school grounds. This conversation will help the children to make the transition to the new unit theme and focus their thinking on the spring season.

The lesson procedures are well detailed, clear, and written so that another teacher could easily follow the sequence and know precisely what to do in teaching the lesson. When writing the procedures, it is useful to include—as this teacher has—some possible reactions of the children, thoughts about what they may do or say or how they may respond to the teacher's directions and questions. Although it is impossible to anticipate every student response, putting oneself in the children's place, *envisioning* their reactions and responses to questions and directions can help to minimize the times when an unusual or distracting response upsets the instructional session. Another value of this exercise is that one is compelled to consider the children's different thinking abilities as an integral part of the lesson planning process.

FIGURE 5.7
A children's concept web
for spring

Final steps in the plan will determine if the children have understood the point of the lesson; that is, if the intended purpose of the introductory lesson has been realized. ***Closure*** is a critical step that needs to be included in any lesson plan. This step is usually at the end of the lesson procedure, and it provides the children with a summary of what they have learned (or for this lesson, what the group has decided). In this lesson, the teacher will need to raise a final question focusing the children's attention on what they will look for while on their walk. This final step in the procedure is included intentionally to leave the children with a plan in mind for their field trip. It will also be at this step that the specific objective—the behavioral objective—of the lesson will be assessed. The following is the behavioral objective for this introductory lesson in the "Spring" unit:

Behavioral Objective

In response to the question, "What signs of spring might we look for as we walk in our school neighborhood?" the children will name at least three items (flowers, animals, budding trees, etc.).

In the behavioral objective, it is clear that the main point of the introductory lesson is to have the children prepared with a purpose for their field trip, with some specific signs of spring to look for while on their neighborhood walk. The behavioral objective will be assessed by asking the question stated in the objective and listing the children's responses on the board. This will be the final step in the procedure; it not only tests the behavioral objective but brings closure to the lesson.

Although the behavioral objective will assess the main purpose of the lesson—to elicit a list of signs of spring the children already know—the teacher will want the children to observe other signs they do not know when the walk is actually taken; otherwise, the activity will not add substantially to the children's existing knowledge.

Step Four: Describing Other Lessons and Activities

Most of the lesson and activity ideas shown in the web are stated so succinctly that the teacher could have difficulty later remembering exactly what he or she had in mind. Therefore, each idea is described in a separate section of the unit plan, where the general idea and purpose of the lesson and activity are stated in greater detail. Three detailed descriptions of ideas shown in the "Spring" web follow. One idea is for painting a mural and several other activities following the children's walk in their neighborhood. There is a description for a lesson on reading a thermometer and one for preparing a learning center.

Descriptions of Lessons and Activities

▩ *On the day the children take their field trip (walk) through their neighborhood to look for signs of spring, stop occasionally and encourage the children to draw or paint one or more sketches showing the signs of spring they notice: animals, birds, insects, etc. Collect specimens of plants and samples of water to take back to the classroom. After returning to the classroom, have some of the sketches transferred (and enlarged)*

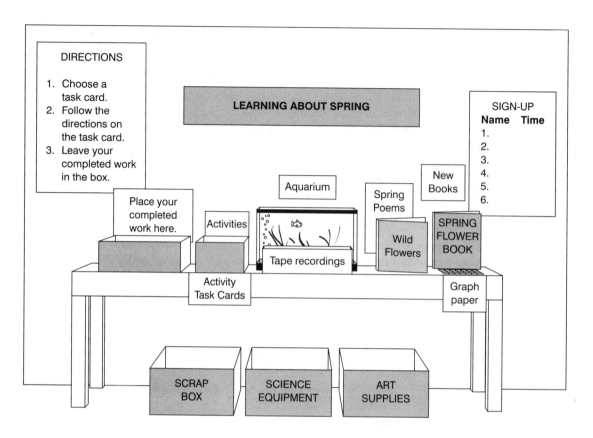

FIGURE 5.8
A model for a "Learning About Spring" learning center

to a large sheet of mural paper. Involve the children in selecting and arranging the pictures on the mural. Some children will be able to use resources in the classroom to determine the names of the plant specimens and to learn more about their growth patterns and needs. One of several learning center activities will have children use a microscope to examine the samples of water brought back from the field trip.

Sketching their observations and collecting samples during the field trip offer children opportunities to be involved in the work of scientists. The children will use art media to prepare the mural, which will develop a visual summary of the signs of spring they observed.

▨ Teach the children how to read an outdoor thermometer. A thermometer will need to be installed outside of a classroom window, and the children will have opportunities to practice reading the temperature.

The purpose of this lesson is to prepare the children for keeping a daily temperature record for two weeks during the spring.

※ *Prepare a learning center with at least 10 activities for the children to complete independently. Activities for the learning center will include examining samples of water taken from various sources during their neighborhood walk and writing about or drawing a picture of what they observe. If frogs' eggs are available during the spring, samples will be collected and placed in the learning center for the children to observe, and they will have an opportunity to read books about the changes involved as the eggs develop into tadpoles and adult frogs. Suggestions will also be included in the center for creative writing of poems and stories about how spring weather affects our feelings. A listening activity, including environmental sounds and musical selections, will also be located in the learning center. There will be mathematical problem solving activities related to the daily temperature charts the children are maintaining. Children will have the option of submitting any responses or records required for the activities either in written or pictorial form. Each activity will have a task card to explain directions.*

The learning center will provide children with independent work to extend practice with the concepts they are studying during the unit in the areas of science, music, language arts, and mathematics. (Figure 5.8 shows a possible way to organize the center.)

The preceding lesson and activity descriptions add to basic information provided in the web and make it easier to design complete plans for the ideas later if the teacher decides to use them. (Additional descriptions can be found in the sample "Spring" unit plan at the end of this chapter.)

Step Five: Listing the General Unit Objectives

While each lesson or activity will have a specific, behaviorally stated objective, the entire unit plan has comprehensive or **general** objectives as well. General objectives are the overall or long-term goals toward which the unit is expected to contribute. They suggest the major purposes for which the unit has been designed, by stating the content it will include as well as the affective and process goals it will help to promote. An example of each type of general objective—content, attitudinal, and process—for the "Spring" unit follows:

General Objectives

Content: To help the children become more aware of the changes going on about them in their environment and to learn more about specific changes during the season of spring.

Attitudinal: To help children appreciate that works of art, music, and literature can be inspired by feelings people associate with seasons of the year.

Process: To give the children opportunities to use media—art, music, movement—to express feelings, attitudes, and ideas.

(Additional general objectives are included in the sample unit plan for "Spring" at the end of this chapter.)

Step Six: Listing Tentative Evaluation Methods and Techniques

Both general and behavioral objectives are helpful in assessing a unit of study; however, unit evaluation usually involves other assessment techniques, such as direct observation of the students' ability to work together, to use equipment properly, and to assess their own work. Portfolio assessment is especially useful in unit evaluation because teachers and children are able to assemble in a student portfolio an authentic record of actual work the student has produced or is involved in developing. The portfolio can include a journal, samples of written work, science experiments, and art the student has produced. Examinations are also useful, especially when added to authentic measures, for assessing each student's progress toward developing the conceptual knowledge the unit has been designed to foster. Descriptions of several evaluation techniques that are planned for the "Spring" unit follow:

Evaluation Techniques

Periodically observe the children during group activities, particularly while they are working on the mural and during planting activities. Watch specifically for their ability to share materials and space. Note those observations in a journal.

Have each child maintain a unit portfolio. Involve individual children in selecting the following materials for their portfolios:

- Samples of written work or work in progress, including creative writing and any written reports
- Examples or photographs of the child's art projects or projects in progress
- A journal maintained by the child, including any observations or notes
- Records of observations and notes made by the teacher
- Records or notes on any individual pupil/teacher conferences
- Records of science experiments completed by the child
- Unit examination

Maintain anecdotal records of observations made about each child's general work habits, working and learning style preferences, cooperation when working with others, and ability to learn through experiential activities.

Keep a journal throughout the unit of work. Include observations of activities and lessons that appear to be most helpful in developing the unit objectives. Also, note the need for revisions in the unit plan, areas that need to be strengthened and additional activities that need to be offered to meet children's individual learning styles.

Administer an examination at the conclusion of the unit to assess facts, concepts, and generalizations developed in the study. The examination will be given orally for children who have difficulty reading the questions. Children should pass the test with a minimum grade of 75 percent.

Step Seven: Listing Essential Materials

In this section of the unit plan, only essential materials need to be listed. Titles of specific books, films, videotapes, and their sources are important to keep on record for future reference, particularly if any have been found to be especially useful or effective. The names of people who have been helpful as consultants or as guest speakers can also be included in this list. Most of the usual art and other consumable materials need not be listed. Each time the unit is taught, new materials will be available and will need to be added to the list. However, when initially preparing a unit, before it is taught for the first time, the materials list can be brief and include only the most important materials. Several examples follow:

Materials

- Videotapes of Nova Nature Programs (in the school media center) and those recorded from Instructional Television (ITV) services
- Filmstrip on planting seeds (in the school media center)
- Recordings of music and environmental sounds
- James Smith (consultant with the local weather TV channel)
- A selection of children's books from the school and public libraries having spring as the theme
- Computer software featuring information on the seasons and nature

Step Eight: Deciding the Unit Title or Designing a Method of Involving the Children in Creating a Title

This final step is an important one, and it can usually be accomplished quite easily. Certainly, "Spring" could be the title of this sample unit. However, children can probably think of a title they like better. Offering the children a chance to suggest their own title is in fact a very good way to stimulate their interest and help them become **invested** in their unit. In reality, the unit belongs to the children, so it is important for them to feel some sense of ownership. The children can also help to prepare the title they select for display in the classroom throughout the study. The title can be made from cut-out letters, written with crayon, painted on a long strip of paper, or made from other suitable materials.

Title

Possible titles

"Spring"

"Signs of Spring"

"Spring Is Here"

"Spring Changes"

Method of Involving Students in Selecting a Title

- The children can suggest other titles during a class meeting, or individual children can write suggested titles and place them in a suggestion box. A class vote can be taken to select the final title.
- Two or three volunteers will be asked to cut letters for the title that will then be displayed at the top of a large bulletin board.

"Spring"—A Sample Thematic Unit Plan

The eight-step process described in the preceding section has generated the material needed to write a formal unit plan and to complete the unit plan outline illustrated in Figure 5.1 at the beginning of this chapter. That outline only reorders the material produced in the eight-step process and provides a logical organizational framework for the plan. The complete "Spring" unit plan follows.

"Spring"—A Thematic Unit Plan (Primary Level)

Theme:	Spring
Estimated Length:	Three to four weeks
Possible titles:	"Spring;" "Spring Is Here;" "Signs of Spring;" "Spring Changes"

Method of Involving Students in Selecting a Title:

- The children can suggest other titles during a class meeting or individual children can write suggested titles and place them in a suggestion box. A class vote can be taken to select the final title.
- Two or three volunteers will be asked to cut letters for the title that will then be displayed at the top of the large bulletin board.

LEVEL: GRADE TWO

This unit plan is designed specifically for children in the second grade, but it can be adapted for students in grades three or four.

GENERAL OBJECTIVES

Content

- To help the children become more aware of the changes going on about them in their environment and to learn more about specific changes during the season of spring.

- To provide children with experiences that will help them to understand that all plants need varying amounts of air, sunlight, and water in order to thrive.

- To introduce children to graphs and their uses in inquiry.

- To help children learn that all sound is produced by vibrating objects.

- To increase the children's knowledge of the various holidays that occur during the spring season and to develop their understanding of the many ways people in our society celebrate those occasions.

- To provide children with experiences that will help them relate the idea that seasonal changes bring about some of the events they can actually observe in their own community.

Attitudinal

- To help children appreciate that works of art, music, and literature can be inspired by feelings people associate with seasons of the year.

- To develop the children's awareness that various phenomena, including the weather and seasonal changes, can affect our feelings and attitudes, and that we may experience changes in feelings because of seasonal changes in our environment.

- To help children appreciate that scientific experimentation demands preciseness and patience.

Process

- To give the children opportunities to use media—art, music, movement— to express feelings, attitudes, and ideas.

- To help children further develop and refine their observational skills.

- To give the children experiences in using instruments and in preparing graphs to record changes they observe.

- To provide opportunities for children to apply the scientific method in experimenting with plants.

- To help children realize that even though scientific investigations may fail to support their hypotheses, it is always possible to learn from the inquiry.

- To provide children with practice in recording data to show the results of their investigations.

DIAGRAM OF THE PLAN

See Figure 5.9.

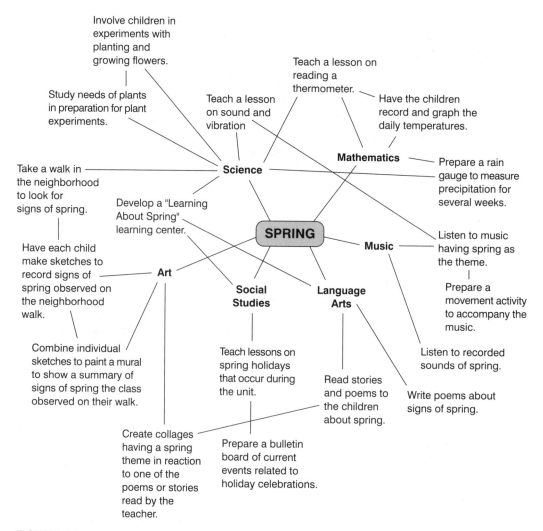

FIGURE 5.9
Diagram for a complete thematic unit plan on "Spring"

INTRODUCTORY LESSON PLAN

Topic:	Unit Theme: "Spring"
	Lesson to prepare children for a walk in their neighborhood to observe signs of spring
Level:	Grade 2
General Objective:	To prepare children for a field excursion to observe signs of spring in the school neighborhood.

Time: 20 to 25 minutes

Behavioral Objective: In response to the question, "What signs of spring might we look for when we take our walk in the neighborhood?" the children will name at least three items (flowers, animals, budding trees, etc.).

Procedure

1. Select a day for the field trip in advance, and secure the necessary permissions. Invite two adults from the list of parent volunteers to assist with supervision while on the walk. (The field trip will be taken after this introductory lesson, which is designed only to prepare the children for their walk.)

2. The first lesson will begin with a class meeting in the early afternoon during the time regularly devoted to unit studies.

3. Begin the lesson by reminding the children that they have studied their neighborhood this year and that their last unit was "Our School." Ask the children to recall some activities from that unit.

   Children will probably say they remember drawing a map of the school, and visiting and interviewing several people who work in the school: the nurse, the school principal, and a custodian. They will also remember learning about the work the people do, that they actually saw where the people do their work, and that they were given a chance to see some materials the people use for their jobs. The children may also recall drawing and labeling pictures of school helpers.

4. Ask the children if they have noticed that the school custodians are beginning to do some work they have not been able to do all winter.

   The children may have noticed that the school custodians are working outside on the grounds.

5. Ask the children if they can think of any reasons why work is beginning outside at this time of year.

   Children will probably say that it is because the grass is growing and that it is warmer. They may also say it is now spring.

6. Tell the children that they will be studying this new season and that "spring" is the theme of their new unit.

7. Ask the children what they already know about the spring season. Write their responses on the board. A concept web will be used to record what the children say.

   Responses may include that it is a special time of the year, a time when the weather gets warmer and they no longer have to wear heavy clothing. They may say that the grass and some flowers begin to grow in the spring and that the trees have buds. Some may remember that there are some important holidays during the spring season.

8. Suggest that all of their ideas are important to have noticed. Then ask the children if they know that their ideas are actually "signs" of the spring season. Write "sign" on the board, and ask if the children know what it means.

   Children will probably say that a sign is a signal or idea of something. Other responses may be given as well.

9. Tell the children that there may actually be many more signs of spring they have not yet noticed, and explain that at the end of the week, the class will take a walk along several streets near the school to look for signs of spring in the neighborhood. Then ask, "What signs of spring might we look for when we take our walk in the neighborhood?" Write any signs the children suggest in a list on a large sheet of paper. The list will be used as a reminder of the signs the children will look for immediately before they leave the classroom on the day of the walk.

   The children will be likely to suggest looking for different kinds of flowers and noticing where the grass has begun to turn green. They may also mention looking for birds that have returned after the winter and examining trees and shrubs for signs of new growth.

10. To conclude the lesson, summarize briefly by reviewing the list of signs of spring on the chart.

11. Finally, distribute permission slips and explain that each person will need to take a permission slip home to be signed and that the slips will need to be returned in two days so the class can take the walk.

Materials

Chart paper and a supply of parental permission slips to distribute to each child in the class.

DESCRIPTIONS OF LESSONS AND ACTIVITIES

• On the day the children take their field trip (walk) through their neighborhood to look for signs of spring, stop occasionally and encourage the children to draw or paint one or more sketches showing the signs of spring they notice: animals, birds, insects, etc. Collect specimens of plants and samples of water to take back to the classroom. After returning to the classroom, have some of the sketches transferred (and enlarged) to a large sheet of mural paper. Involve the children in selecting and arranging the pictures on the mural. Some children will be able to use resources in the classroom to determine the names of the plant specimens and to learn more about their growth patterns and needs. One of several learning center activities will have children use a microscope to examine the samples of water brought back from the field trip.

  Sketching their observations and collecting samples during the field trip offer children opportunities to be involved in the work of scientists. The children will use art media to prepare the mural, which will develop a visual summary of the signs of spring they observed.

- Teach the children how to read an outdoor thermometer. A thermometer will need to be installed outside of a classroom window, and the children will have opportunities to practice reading the thermometer.

   The purpose of this lesson is to prepare the children for keeping a daily temperature record for two weeks during the spring.

- Help the children make a rain gauge. Locate the gauge in an outdoor area near the classroom for the children to inspect after any precipitation. Then prepare a chart showing the amount of precipitation each week throughout the unit. The different amounts can be used to create addition and subtraction problems to solve in mathematics.

   This activity will provide children with opportunities to observe, measure, create a graph, and practice computation skills.

- Have the children use their daily temperature records for a lesson on graphing. Work with the children to prepare a simple graph (either line or bar) to chart the temperature readings children have recorded.

   The purpose of this mathematics lesson is to introduce the children to graphing and to help them develop a record of one change the spring season brings.

- If plant specimens have been collected from the field trip, some children may want to care for those plants. The children can determine what each plant needs, care for it, and keep a record to show how the plant changes throughout the spring.

- Give the children opportunities to conduct their own experiments to determine the basic needs of plants. Begin by having the children suggest what plants need in order to live, and then help them to set up experiments to test their ideas. Some of the children will already know what plants need to live; they can use scientific experiments to confirm what they believe. Some children may fail to control variables in conducting their experiments. When this happens, let the children perform their experiments, then raise questions to help them realize the need to test one variable at a time. Replicate experiments when needed.

   The purpose of the experiments is not only to help children discover the basic needs of the plants they use but also to give the children opportunities to design and carry out their own scientific investigations.

- After children determine, experimentally, the basic needs of plants, teach a lesson on planting flower seeds. Use marigold seeds because they will grow rapidly and easily under proper conditions. In this activity, the children should decide the conditions needed for growing the seeds and be given time to collect soil and containers for the growing plants. Ask the children to observe the plants each day and keep a record by writing or drawing the changes they observe. The children should also measure and chart the height of their plants each week after the seeds have sprouted. Later in the spring, the children can take their plants home when the marigolds are mature enough for transplanting.

The purpose of this science activity is give the children a "hands-on" experience in raising and care for growing plants.

• Prepare a learning center with at least 10 activities for the children to complete independently. Activities for the learning center will include examining samples of water taken from various sources during their neighborhood walk and writing about or drawing a picture of what they observe. If frogs' eggs are available during the spring, samples will be collected and placed in the learning center for the children to observe, and they will have an opportunity to read books about the changes involved as the eggs develop into tadpoles and adult frogs. Suggestions will also be included in the center for creative writing of poems and stories about how spring weather affects our feelings. A listening activity, including environmental sounds and musical selections, will also be located in the learning center. There will be mathematical problem solving activities related to the daily temperature charts the children are maintaining. Children will have the option of submitting any responses or records required for the activities either in written or pictorial form. Each activity will have a task card to explain directions.

The learning center will provide children with independent work to extend practice with the concepts they are studying during the unit in the areas of science, music, language arts, and mathematics.

• Conduct several lessons on sound. Begin with a listening exercise by having the children listen to a tape recording of spring sounds in their environment. The children should try to identify sounds of birds chirping, children playing outside, water rushing in a stream, etc. Next, select recordings of music having spring as the theme. Try to include both classical and popular music, and have the children listen for specific feelings the music creates for them individually. Discuss those feelings, and give children the choice of either writing their feelings in their journals, or creating poetry or drawings to represent their feelings. These listening activities can lead to a lesson on what causes sound.

The main purpose of this activity is to develop children's auditory sense and discrimination, to introduce them to the concept that all sound is caused by vibration, and to help them to realize that the sounds we hear can stimulate different feelings.

• Give lessons on spring holidays that occur during the unit. Select appropriate stories and video, film, and filmstrip presentations about the holidays to use in the lessons. Conduct these lessons as directed listening or viewing activities. Provide a purpose for listening or viewing, then raise questions about the reading or media presentation at the end of the activity. Keep the lessons quite informal, emphasizing the information provided in each about a particular holiday.

The purpose of these social studies lessons will be to provide the children with insights about how each of the holidays came about and the different ways that people in our multicultural society celebrate those holidays.

- Prepare a spring holiday current events bulletin board. Invite the children to look through the magazines and newspapers in the classroom to find articles and pictures showing spring holiday celebrations. The local newspaper will mean most to the children because it will have items on local events with which the children are more likely to be familiar. Invite children to write their own articles or create drawings that describe the current events that are especially important to them. Collect items for the display, and have several children decide how to place them on the bulletin board. Hold a discussion of the items on the bulletin board with the class.

   The discussion of the events should help the children to realize that there are activities in their own community that are related to the changes that come about during the spring season.

- Have the children prepare collages on the spring theme. They can use the holidays, signs of spring, spring plants, or other ideas they may have to create their art. As an alternative, some children may want to write a song or create a dance to express their feelings or new learnings about changes that occur during the spring season.

   The purpose of this activity is to give the children opportunities to express their creativity and to work with various art media (or music or movement).

- Periodically, throughout the unit on spring, select and read to the children stories, books, and poems having the changes that occur in the spring season as a theme. The readings should lead to one or more lessons in which children write their own stories or poems about spring or prepare drawings to express their thoughts.

   The purpose of these listening and creative activities is to give children opportunities to express themselves using a variety of forms.

EVALUATION TECHNIQUES

- Periodically observe the children during group activities, particularly while they are working on the mural and during planting activities. Watch specifically for their ability to share materials and space. Note those observations in a journal.

- Have each child maintain a unit portfolio. Involve individual children in selecting the following materials for their portfolios:

   Samples of written work or work in progress, including creative writing and any written reports

   Examples or photographs of the child's art projects or projects in progress

   A journal maintained by the child, including any observations or notes

   Records of observations and notes made by the teacher

   Records or notes on any individual pupil/teacher conferences

   Records of science experiments completed by the child

   Unit examination

- Maintain anecdotal records of observations made about each child's general work habits, working and learning style preferences, cooperation when working with others, and ability to learn through experiential activities.

- Keep a journal throughout the unit of work. Include observations of activities and lessons that appear to be most helpful in developing the unit objectives. Also, note the need for revisions in the unit plan, areas that need to be strengthened, and additional activities that need to be offered to meet children's individual learning styles.

- Administer a short examination at the conclusion of the unit to assess facts, concepts, and generalizations developed in the study. The examination will be given orally for children who have difficulty reading the questions.

MATERIALS

- Videotapes of Nova Nature Programs (in the school media center) and those recorded from Instructional Television (ITV) services

- Filmstrip on planting seeds (in the school media center)

- Filmstrip on needs of plants (to show after children conduct their own experiments with plants)

- Materials for experiments with plants

- Recordings of music and environmental sounds

- James Smith (consultant with the local weather TV channel)

- A selection of children's books from the school and public libraries having spring as the theme

- Computer software featuring information on the seasons and nature

- Marigold (or other annual) seeds for planting

- Tuning fork for the lesson on vibration

- Tape recording of spring sounds (homemade)

The "Spring" unit plan is the only complete thematic unit for an early childhood grade level included in this book. In the appendix, readers will find additional graphic webs showing the designs for 14 thematic units that can be adapted for teaching at different grade levels.

References

Armstrong, T. (1994). *Multiple intelligences in the classroom.* Alexandria, VA: Association for Supervision and Curriculum Development.

Charbonneau, M. P., & Reider, B. E. (1995). *The integrated elementary classroom: A developmental model of education for the 21st century.* Needham Heights, MA: Allyn & Bacon.

Ellis, A. K. (1995). *Teaching and learning elementary social studies* (5th ed.). Boston: Allyn & Bacon.

Fredericks, A. D., & Cheesebrough, D. L. (1993). *Science for all children.* New York: Harper Collins.

Jacobs, H. (Ed.). (1989). *Interdisciplinary curriculum: Design and implementation.* Alexandria, VA: Association for Supervision and Curriculum Development.

Kauchak, D. P., & Eggen, P. D. (1993). *Learning and teaching* (2nd ed.). Boston: Allyn & Bacon.

McNeil, J. D., & Wiles, J. (1990). *The essentials of teaching: Decisions, plans, methods.* New York: Macmillan.

Pappas, C. C., Kiefer, B. Z., & Levstik, L. S. (1995). *An integrated language perspective in the elementary school.* White Plains, NY: Longman.

Roberts, P. L., & Kellough, R. D. (1996). *A guide for developing an interdisciplinary thematic unit.* Upper Saddle River, NJ: Merrill/Prentice Hall.

Stephens, L. S. (1974). *The teacher's guide to open education.* New York: Holt, Rinehart & Winston.

Suggested Readings

Katz, L., & Chard, S. C. (1989). *Engaging children's minds: The project approach.* Norwood, NJ: Ablex Publishing.

Reigeluth, C. M. (1987). *Instructional theories in action: Lessons illustrating selected theories and models.* Hillsdale, NJ: Erlbaum.

Sava, S. G. (1975). *Learning through discovery for young children.* New York: McGraw-Hill.

Torbert, W. R. (1972). *Learning from experience: Toward consciousness.* New York: Columbia University Press.

Wadsworth, B. J. (1978). *Piaget for the classroom teacher.* New York: Longman.

6

Designing Research-Oriented Thematic Units for Intermediate and Middle School Grades

An eight-step procedure for planning a research-oriented thematic unit for students in the intermediate grades and middle school is described and illustrated in this chapter. The chapter includes:

- *An introduction to research-oriented thematic units, explaining how these unit plans differ from other thematic units, along with reasons why research-oriented thematic units offer a developmentally appropriate alternative type of interdisciplinary study for older students.*
- *An outline for a research-oriented thematic unit plan and a list indicating the information to be included under each heading in the plan.*
- *An eight-step procedure for planning a research-oriented thematic unit.*
- *An explanation of each step with examples from a unit on "Deserts of the United States," which is being planned for students in an intermediate grade.*
- *A complete sample unit plan on "Deserts of the United States."*
- *A method for modifying research-oriented thematic units for a departmentalized intermediate or middle school program.*

At the intermediate and middle school levels, a different type of interdisciplinary unit, the **research-oriented thematic unit,** can be planned as an alternative to the thematic units described in Chapter 5. Research-oriented thematic units differ from thematic units in several ways:

- Students work individually and also serve on committees or small, cooperative groups.
- The central theme of the unit is separated into component subtopics for the committees to research.
- Each student assumes the responsibility for a specific part of his/her committee's research.
- Written research reports—or alternate methods of reporting—are prepared by individual students and the committees.
- Each committee summarizes its part of the research for the entire class in an oral presentation.
- The research process guides the development of the unit and its procedures.
- Students become actively involved in developing questions and suggesting areas to be researched in their unit.

In research-oriented thematic units, students work on individual and/or group projects and have opportunities to continue improving their research and other academic skills. They also gain added insights about the ways of knowing inherent in the different disciplines they use in their investigation of the theme. Students work independently, in small cooperative groups, or as members of **committees** to complete their research. In middle childhood and early adolescence, students thoroughly enjoy participating in group activities with their peers. Therefore, the committee work in a research-oriented thematic unit is appealing and naturally motivating. Practical guidance on the type of cooperative grouping involved in committee work at elementary and middle school levels can be found in *Cooperative Learning in the Classroom* (Johnson, Johnson, & Holubec, 1994) and two especially helpful publications from the National Education Association (Lyman, Foyle, & Azwell, 1993; Rottier & Ogan, 1991).

Most students in the intermediate grades and middle school will have developed adequate research, reading, and writing skills for the academic work required in research-oriented thematic units, and teachers can usually find more independent-level reading and other resource materials prepared on topics for older students to use for their research. It is important to note, however, that not *all* older students may be ready for the work involved in this type of unit. Therefore, teachers who know their students have difficulty with reading and writing skills should follow the procedure outlined in Chapter 5 for thematic units, mainly because those plans do not demand the same level of independence in linguistic skills.

Research-Oriented Thematic Unit Plan Outline

The eight-step procedure explained and illustrated in the next section will provide the information needed to complete the outline for a research-oriented thematic unit plan. The outline is shown in Figure 6.1.

The format includes the usual objectives, procedures to be followed, important materials, and evaluation techniques. In addition, several specific elements required only for this type of interdisciplinary unit plan are included. Major headings, along with statements indicating the planning task and information needed for each section, are outlined as follows:

Topic or Theme

State the theme of the unit.

Estimated Length

Estimate the amount of time needed to teach the unit.

Title

List suggestions for a title and possible ways to involve students in selecting a title for the unit.

FIGURE 6.1
A research-oriented thematic
unit plan outline

Topic or Theme:

Estimated Length:

Title:

Level:

General Objectives:

Diagram of the Plan:

Possible Research Committees:

Sample Questions to Guide Students' Research:

Possible Unit Activities and Lessons:

Introductory Lesson in the Planning Phase:

 Topic:

 Level:

 General Objective:

 Time:

 Behavioral Objective:

 Procedure:

 Materials:

Description of the Remainder of the Planning Phase:

Description of the Research Phase:

Description of the Reporting Phase:

Evaluation Techniques:

Materials:

Level

State the grade or grades for which the unit is intended, keeping in mind the students' background and readiness for the unit, their social and developmental characteristics, and their academic abilities.

General Objectives

List general cognitive, affective, and learning process objectives for the unit. These objectives suggest major areas the unit is designed to promote, including concepts, attitudes, and processes of learning.

Diagram of the Plan

Construct a web showing research activities, skills lessons, and other related activity ideas.

Possible Research Committees

List several subtopics of the unit that might be assigned to groups of students for committee research.

Sample Questions to Guide Students' Research

Prepare lists of questions for the various disciplines that may help to guide the research in the committees. The questions to be listed in this section are mainly to help the teacher prepare a framework for the unit; the students will be encouraged to generate their own questions and problem statements for their research.

Possible Unit Activities and Lessons

Describe several possible research and reporting alternatives that students may be able to use in connection with their committee or individual research. Lessons that will need to be taught—those included in the web design—should also be described in this section. Try to make provisions for students' differing working and learning styles, and their multiple intelligences.

Introductory Lesson (or Session) in the Planning Phase

This lesson plan will outline a procedure for the first session. It needs to assist students in planning for their research. Although other lesson plan formats can be substituted for the one given here, the plan must be able to accommodate information included in the following outline.

Topic: State the unit theme and the topic of the lesson.

Level: State the age level(s) or grade(s) for which the lesson is designed.

General Objective(s): State one or more general objectives for the lesson.

Time: Estimate the amount of time that will be needed for the first session in planning for student research.

Behavioral Objective(s): State the specific objective(s) for the initial procedure in the planning phase of the unit.

Procedure: Write a paragraph or a sequential list of steps detailing the procedure for the initial session in this phase. Include anticipated student responses when appropriate.

Materials: List the essential materials needed for the session.

Description of the Remainder of the Planning Phase

Describe how the planning phase will be completed after the initial session. This phase ends with the formation of committees, and outlining and reaching agreement on individual student responsibilities.

Description of the Research Phase

Describe the activities that will take place as students pursue their individual projects and committee research.

Description of the Reporting Phase

Explain the procedure and describe possible reporting alternatives for the student committee reports. It is important to keep in mind students' different learning and working styles and to provide for some variety in reporting methods.

Evaluation Techniques

List overall unit evaluation techniques, such as portfolios to be assembled during the unit and examinations to be administered, in addition to measures described in the behavioral objectives for lesson and activity plans.

Materials

List materials needed for the unit. Include general kinds of films, video and computer software programs, filmstrips, texts and trade books, magazines, and newspapers. Each time the unit is taught to a new group of students, specific titles found to be especially valuable, along with notes or descriptions of their contents, can be added to the general list. Some materials may need to be updated or deleted from the list of materials each time the unit is used with a new group.

An Eight-Step Procedure for Developing Research-Oriented Thematic Unit Plans

Themes selected for the intermediate grades and middle school should be kept broad in scope in order to increase opportunities for student participation. Excellent planning guides developed by the National Council for the Social Studies can help to guide the selection process. However, themes can emanate from disciplines other than those included in the social studies curriculum. Humphreys, Post, and Ellis (1981) recommend selecting themes with an environmental focus. Environmental themes are of interest to most students in the intermediate grades and middle school, and they always involve several disciplines. In long-term planning, teachers will need to consult statewide and local curriculum requirements before making decisions about the list of themes to be taught throughout the academic year. Often, there is a prescribed course of study, especially for the middle school (Kellough & Kellough, 1996). Several criteria can be especially helpful in making final decisions about themes to teach:

- The theme should be broad and inclusive in scope. However, time constraints for teaching the unit, if any, need to be taken into consideration because they may influence the type of theme that can be investigated.
- Themes required by the state should be included where they fit most naturally.
- Consider the availability of resource materials needed by students to investigate the theme; materials the students will need to read should be written at their independent reading levels.
- The theme should involve as many disciplines as possible.
- In order to be sufficiently motivating, whenever it is feasible, a theme should be of inherent interest to the students. The theme selected should also be flexible enough to allow for differences in individual interests and styles of learning.
- A theme should help to broaden students' understanding of our multicultural world and strengthen their sense of social responsibility.

After selecting a theme, the following eight steps are suggested for planning a research-oriented thematic unit:

1. Consider the students' developmental abilities and their background for the theme.
2. Brainstorm to develop four lists: possible committees, questions to help guide students' research, other unit activities, and skills lessons to be taught during the unit. (An optional diagram—or web—showing the unit design can be constructed.)
3. Plan the initial lesson to be held with students. This first lesson—or session— introduces the critical *planning phase* of the unit.
4. Write a description of the general procedure to be followed in completing the three phases of the unit: the planning, research, and reporting phases.
5. List general objectives for the unit.
6. List tentative evaluation methods and techniques.
7. List essential materials.
8. Decide the unit title, or develop a method for involving students in deciding a title of their own.

In addition to drafting a web of ideas, the second step in designing a research-oriented thematic unit involves preparing four resource lists: (1) a list of *committees* that might be formed to investigate the theme, (2) a list of *questions* to help guide students' research, (3) a list giving brief *descriptions of activities*, and (4) a list of specific *skills lessons* to be taught during the unit. The same chart of disciplines, study areas, and techniques used in thematic unit planning can also be helpful when preparing these four lists. (That chart is shown in Chapter 5, Figure 5.4.)

An explanation of the eight-step procedure for planning a research-oriented thematic unit follows. The examples given at each step are from an intermediate-grade research unit plan on the theme, "Deserts of the United States." (Only a few examples from the complete unit plan are given at each of the steps. The complete unit plan can be found on pages 98–111 in this chapter, following the explanation of the eight-step procedure.)

Step One: Considering the Students' Developmental Abilities and Background

In the intermediate grades and middle school, most students like to work together, their thinking has matured, and their academic skills have developed so that they can do more of their work independently. The teacher will keep this information in mind as planning begins for a fourth-grade research-oriented unit. The following class description includes a number of important points about this particular group of students:

The children in this heterogeneous group of fourth graders should have opportunities for direct experiences whenever possible to help them develop concepts to be fostered in their "Desert" unit. Independent reading levels in the class range from second to eighth grade; it has been found that the children vary in their individual learning and working styles. Several children are especially talented in art. The children have had experience working in committees; they work well in these cooperative groups, provided the tasks are clear and well outlined and there is some leadership in each group. Guidance is needed when the children use the library for research, and they are learning about taking notes when reading for information. The class includes the usual personality conflicts that occasionally emerge in groups at this level, and there are minor behavior problems at times. Those problems are less pronounced when the children become interested and involved in their work. There are three special needs children in the class; at this point, one child is not able to read well enough independently for information, another child has been diagnosed with minimal brain damage, and one student has only residual hearing. Although they will all be able to participate in committee work, they will require more time for their work and will need to have opportunities to learn through alternative strategies. Interviews, drawings, tape recordings, videotaped presentations, and computer software may be helpful. Recently, the class has completed a unit on their local Long Island and New York City coastal region. Children are beginning to realize how geographical location can affect people. They are also learning more about the concept of interdependence.

The description reviews both the group and the children's individual characteristics, and their academic and social skills. While planning and introducing the unit, the teacher will keep in mind the previous unit theme, the children's background, and their strengths and limitations.

Step Two: Brainstorming to Develop Four Lists, and Preparing the Graphic Design for the Unit

A design—or web—similar to those used for other thematic units can be constructed for research-oriented thematic units. If a web is constructed for the unit, it is recommended that the theme be stated boldly, with research committees, activities, specific skills lessons, and other related class activities stated very briefly and radiating from the theme. Lines are then drawn to show how the disciplines, lessons, and activities interrelate.

There is no one *correct* way to design the web. Different web designs, each of which is appropriate for research-oriented thematic unit plans, are shown in Roberts and Kellough (1996); Pappas, Kiefer, and Levstik (1995); Ellis (1995); Charbonneau and Reider (1995); and Jacobs (1989). A partially completed web for the "Deserts" unit is shown in Figure 6.2.

Most teachers will prefer to develop lists in addition to—or perhaps instead of—drawing a web, mainly because the design for a research unit web can become crowded, and it is time-consuming to diagram. Four lists are developed during the brainstorming step, even when a diagram is constructed. The following examples show the kinds of information in the lists that have been prepared for the "Deserts" unit. (It is important to realize that none of the lists is complete here; the complete "Deserts" unit plan can be found in the sample research-oriented thematic unit plan following the explanation of the eight-step procedure.)

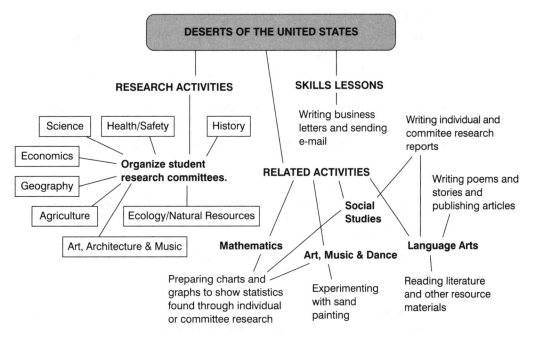

FIGURE 6.2
A partially completed design for the research-oriented thematic unit, "Deserts of the United States"

Possible Committees

Geography	Art/Architecture and Music	History
Health/Safety	Ecology and Natural Resources	Science

Sample Questions to Guide Student Research

The following sample questions are separated by discipline or domain to indicate some of the questions the teacher hopes children will investigate in those areas as they research the theme. Certainly, from an interdisciplinary perspective, the separation is somewhat artificial, mainly because the disciplines and questions will relate to one another and will need to be considered in combinations by the children in the actual inquiry.

Geography

*   How do we define a desert region?
*   How were our deserts formed? How old are they?
*   What are common features of deserts, and what defines a desert area?
*   Where are deserts in the United States located?
*   What are the sizes of deserts in the United States?
*   Are all deserts in the United States alike in some ways? In what ways do they differ from one another?

History

*   Who were the first settlers in deserts of the United States? Why did they initially settle in those areas?
*   How have historians and other social scientists learned about early people who lived in our desert regions?
*   How have artifacts found in our deserts contributed to our understanding of early civilizations?
*   Which Native American tribes currently live in United States desert areas?

Science

*   What animals and plants live in desert areas? Do the same kinds of animals and plants live in all deserts? What are the reasons for any variations found in wildlife in the different deserts?
*   How are desert plants and animals adapted to desert living conditions?

Economics

*   What minerals and other natural resources are found in desert areas; what effects do those resources have on desert society?

- How do people living today in desert areas earn a living?

Agriculture

- Is farming possible in desert areas? If so, what kinds of farms are found in those regions?
- What problems are faced by farmers in those areas?

Art and Architecture

- What famous artists have lived and worked in desert areas? Why do they live there? How can their art be distinguished?

Health

- What kinds of health care are available to people living in sparsely populated desert regions?
- What are the effects of desert climate on the health of people who live in those areas?

Possible Unit Activities and Lessons

- Form research committees.

  There will be a committee for each area shown in the web. Each committee will have four to six children.

  After they have completed their research, the committees will be responsible for reporting their findings to the class.

- Provide for individual inquiry.

  In addition to the subtopics being investigated by the committees, some children may have interests in subtopics that do not relate well to any committee's work.

  Encourage those individuals to pursue their interests, and provide opportunities for them to report their findings to the class.

- Clarify reporting requirements for committees and individuals.

  Require each student to prepare a report of his/her committee research. Those who are capable of writing their reports will be asked to prepare their reports in writing. Provide the children with a form to guide their writing.

- Teach notetaking skills lessons.

- Teach lessons on writing letters and communicating with e-mail.

- Offer individuals and the committees suggestions for alternative research and reporting activities.

  The list includes suggestions that can be made to committees and individual children as the unit progresses. Activities address children's differing working and learning styles.

Suggestions

Compose and send a letter via e-mail to the children in a fourth grade class in a desert region. Ask what it is like to live in a desert region of the United States.

Choose a story or poem on desert life from our classroom collection or from the school media center. Prepare to read it to a group of children in a kindergarten or first grade.

Publish an article (using the computer) comparing living in a desert area with our area.

Organize a panel discussion to present information your group has gained from its research.

Develop a time line to display in the classroom. Use *Timeliner*, if you would like, to prepare it. The time line should indicate the average rainfall each year for the past 10 or more years in a specific desert area.

Develop a plan for an ideal desert house. Make a drawing of the plan.

Create a graph showing some statistics, such as population changes, elevations, or average daily temperature readings, about one of the desert areas you or your committee has been studying.

Try sand painting. We can arrange with our art teacher to help those who would like to try this unique art form.

Invite several classmates to design and paint a mural on life in the desert. (The mural theme can involve animal and plant life, types of homes, typical desert scenes, or other ideas the children suggest.)

Build a model of a Native American community found in one of the desert areas studied.

Prepare a puppet show or present a skit to the class that includes information about some of the effects new settlers had on Native Americans who were living in a desert area.

Collect several recordings that have been written about desert living. Present the songs to the class.

Create a musical instrument made from materials that would be found in a desert. Demonstrate the instrument for the class.

Work with several others to plan a classroom "museum" display of all the projects children in the class have created during the unit. Invite all children in the class to contribute their projects for the display. We can arrange to have other classes in the school visit the museum.

Maintain a journal throughout the unit to record your thoughts and feelings related to our study of deserts.

Step Three: Planning the Introductory Lesson

The procedure for a research-oriented thematic unit is outlined very clearly in three phases. A **planning** phase introduces the theme and provides the children with opportunities to participate in organizing for the research they will undertake. This phase is completed when small research committees have been formed to investigate each subtopic of the study. Second, a **researching** phase gives the children time to do their research. During this phase, the teacher oversees each committee's work to ensure that each student is contributing to the group and that children have materials they need for their research and projects. Finally, the unit culminates in a **reporting** phase as committees report their findings to the class. Following each committee report, concepts the group has contributed are outlined by the class.

The first lesson introduces the research theme of the unit and begins the planning phase. In keeping with the general principles of learning (as outlined in Chapter 3), the first lesson in a research unit is designed to help the children form a connection between what they have studied previously and the new theme to be researched. Each step in the lesson procedure should be well detailed and carefully sequenced. In the initial lesson plan, the teacher intentionally poses some questions to stimulate interest and establish a need for the new research. The lesson plan should include the questions to be raised along with responses the teacher anticipates from the children. Part of the procedure and the behavioral objective for the first lesson in the "Deserts" unit follows.

Procedure

1. Before beginning the unit with the children, contact the school librarian, local community children's librarian, and the art and music teachers to let them know the theme of the new unit and to invite their help during the study.

   Librarians can probably assign blocks of books or other media to the class for use during the unit. The community librarian may be able to arrange a display of materials and reserve them for the children in the class during the researching phase. The art and music teachers may be able to develop lessons related to the desert theme.

2. In addition to the social studies, science, and mathematics textbooks available in the classroom, display a sampling of library books, magazines, charts, maps, and other research materials that have been brought from the two libraries. Keep the display small so the children will be motivated to locate other materials themselves.

3. At the first class session, remind the children of the unit they have recently completed on their local region and the Atlantic Coast, and review some of the major concepts they gained from that study.

   The children should recall that coastal areas are important contributors to our inland areas. The natural harbors along the coast have served for many years as major sites for importing goods from all over the world—especially New York Harbor in the children's immediate area. Children will mention the fishing industry and will recall that there is a concentration of population along the Atlantic Coast.

4. Explain that the new unit will be a study of deserts in the United States and that it will focus on life in desert areas and ways people are affected by desert living.

5. Ask the children what they know about deserts, and construct a concept web to record their responses on the chalkboard and later transfer to a chart. (See Figure 5.7 in Chapter 5 for an example of a concept web.) The chart can be modified as the children gain new information; they may need to delete inaccuracies in their original ideas and add other concepts discovered through their studies.

6. Tell the children they will be helping to plan the study and that the first step is to skim available research materials to learn the kinds of information they will be able to find using available resources.

7. Direct the children's attention to the small classroom display of books, magazines, and other materials on deserts in the United States. Explain that these materials have been brought into the classroom for use during the unit and that additional sources will need to be located, some of which are available in the school media center.

8. Ask for three or four volunteers to go to the school library to meet with the librarian who will assist them in locating other materials for the classroom. Have the class secretary keep a list of volunteers' names. Ask one of the volunteers to go to the library to speak to the librarian about a suitable time.

9. Ask the class if anyone can think of sources, other than libraries, where information about deserts in the United States might be found.

   The children will probably mention travel agencies, public television programs, computer programs and the Internet, state agencies, and chambers of commerce in desert areas.

Behavioral Objective

After the teacher introduces the theme of the new unit and directs children's attention to research materials in the classroom, each student will develop a list of the *kinds of information* about deserts in the United States to be found in available materials.

The lesson begins with a review to help children make the transition from their previous study of the Atlantic Coast to the new unit, "Deserts in the United States." They will then develop a concept web to indicate what they know about deserts before beginning their inquiry. Preparing a small display of materials on deserts before beginning the lesson can help to stimulate interest in the new theme. Some children will want to look through the books and magazines even before the introductory lesson is given. The teacher has purposely brought only a few materials to the classroom to allow the children to locate most of their own reference materials. In creating an ad hoc group to search for more materials in the school library, the teacher has already involved the children in the business of the study. Gradually, the children will take over more responsibilities.

The behavioral objective will be realized later in the introductory lesson after the children have had several days to examine resource materials in their classroom.

Step Four: Describing the Remainder of the Planning Phase, and the Research and Reporting Phases

In this step, the teacher describes the procedure to follow in completing the planning phase, then writes a description of each of the phases to follow. These descriptions will guide the remaining procedures for the unit, including its culmination.

Description of the Remainder of the Planning Phase

1. After a composite list of the kinds of information included in available resources has been compiled, duplicated, and distributed to the class, elicit the children's help in organizing general categories from the items on the list. For example, *temperature*, *climate*, *rainfall*, and *wind* may all be included. They can be combined to form the general category—or subtopic—*weather*. Develop an outline with the children of all the subtopics, and have the class secretary copy it for duplication.

2. Duplicate and distribute the outline to each student in the class. Ask each student to list three choices of subtopics for a committee assignment on a slip of paper. Collect the requests and prepare a list of committee assignments.

   The committee assignments should be made with consideration for the social makeup, leadership, and heterogeneity of each group. It will be important to ensure that individuals work on different kinds of committees throughout the year. For example, a student should not always be assigned to the economics committee or the art committee. Final committee assignments are made by the teacher. If any important subtopic is not selected by anyone, several children can be asked if they will form that specific committee, or the teacher can assume responsibility for that area.

3. The committee assignments should then be duplicated and distributed to each child, and the first meeting of committees should be announced. Before committees meet, discuss the meaning of "committee" and how a committee should function. At the first meeting, each committee should select a chairperson and recorder, and the children should decide how they will divide the committee responsibilities among them. The recorder should be directed to write this information for the teacher. In that way, the teacher will know what each student in the class is investigating. The planning phase ends after the initial committee meetings.

Research and Reporting Phases

This part of the unit plan is completed by adding descriptions of the research and reporting phases of the unit; these can be found in the complete "Deserts" unit plan on pages 108–109.

Step Five: Listing the General Unit Objectives

General objectives in this step address the development of children's cognitive, affective, and process skills that will be fostered in the unit study. These objectives are broad in scope and are not usually stated in behavioral terminology. Two examples of general objectives, one cognitive and one in the affective domain, follow.

General Objectives

Cognitive Objective

The children will gain insights about the effect of climate and weather on plant and animal life in desert areas of the United States.

Affective Objective

The children will develop a greater appreciation for the struggles of early desert settlers in adapting to life in desert areas in the United States.

Step Six: Listing Tentative Evaluation Methods and Techniques

In Chapter 5, it was explained that behavioral objectives are useful for evaluating specific lessons and activities. Most teachers in the intermediate and middle school grades will also want to observe the children's ability to cooperate with one another, especially as they work in committees. Direct observation can also help in noting children's progress in applying the academic skills they need for their research. Portfolios, which are discussed in Chapter 4 and are used as an evaluation tool in the thematic unit on "Spring" in Chapter 5, can be especially valuable for assessment of individual children's progress throughout a research-oriented thematic unit. Comprehensive unit examinations, based on the committee presentations, are usually administered at the end of the unit. Sample evaluation statements for this sixth step are listed below.

Evaluation Techniques

- Use observation and maintain a journal during the unit to note children's individual progress in organizing, sharing responsibilities, and participating in committee work.
- Take photographs of the children's art projects as they develop during the unit.
- Have each student maintain a unit portfolio that includes the following materials:

  A file of notes taken for individual research

  Samples of written work or work in progress, including letters, creative writing, and written reports

  Samples or photographs of art projects, constructions, charts or graphs, or works in progress

  A journal reflecting on the student's own work during the unit

  Records of experiments children have designed and completed

  Records or notes on any individual pupil/teacher conferences

  Unit examination

- Collect children's portfolios and add notes about each student's work habits and ability to work with others cooperatively.
- Administer a comprehensive examination at the end of the unit to evaluate the children's mastery of major concepts developed in the unit of study.

Step Seven: Listing Essential Materials

When planning research units, it is most important to keep a list of general categories of available materials, such as types of books, films, videotape programs, and computer software programs on the unit theme. Names of consultants who have been especially helpful can be added to this section after the unit has been taught at least one time. An example follows:

Materials

Social studies and science textbooks from a variety of publishers should be available in sufficient quantities; four to six copies of each textbook are adequate.

Step Eight: Deciding the Unit Title, or Developing a Method for Involving Students in Creating a Title

List any title suggestions for the unit in this step. It is wise to involve the students in creating the title if possible, and it should be displayed prominently in the classroom throughout the study as a reminder for the class and to inform visitors. The following are examples:

Title

Possible Titles:

"Deserts of the United States"

"Our Unusual Desert Areas"

Method of Involving Students in Selecting a Title:

Prepare a suggestion box during the first week of the planning phase of the unit. Children will be asked to contribute title suggestions written on slips of paper. The class officers (president, vice president, and secretary) will choose three title suggestions to present to the class for a vote at the end of the week.

"Deserts of the United States"—A Sample Research-Oriented Thematic Unit Plan

After completing the eight steps detailed in the preceding section, the material that has been generated will help the teacher to estimate the length of the unit. Research-oriented thematic units often last from four to six weeks or more. The information developed in the eight-step procedure can then be reordered and written using the formal unit plan outline shown at the beginning of this chapter. The completed plan for the "Deserts of the United States" unit follows.

"Deserts of the United States"—
A Research-Oriented Thematic Unit Plan
Intermediate to Early Middle School Levels

Topic: Desert Areas of the United States

Estimated Length: Four to six weeks

Possible titles: "Deserts of the United States"; "Our Unusual Desert Areas"

Method of Involving Students in Selecting a Title:

Prepare a suggestion box during the first week of the planning phase of the unit. Children will be asked to contribute title suggestions written on slips of paper. The class officers (president, vice-president, and secretary) will choose three title suggestions to present to the class for a vote at the end of the week.

LEVEL: GRADE FOUR

This unit plan is designed specifically for children in the fourth grade, but it can be adapted for students in the fifth, sixth, or seventh grades.

GENERAL OBJECTIVES

Cognitive Objectives

*   To help develop understandings of the history and economics of development in desert areas of the United States and the effects of development on Native Americans, the first settlers.
*   The children will gain insights about the effect of geography, climate, and weather on human, plant, and animal life in desert areas of the United States.
*   To help children develop an awareness of the effects of the topography and climate in desert areas on art, architecture, music, and literature of the people who live there.

Affective Objective

*   The children will develop a greater appreciation for the struggles of early desert settlers in adapting to life in desert areas in the United States.

DIAGRAM OF THE PLAN

See Figure 6.3.

POSSIBLE RESEARCH COMMITTEES

Geography	Art/Architecture and Music	History
Health/Safety	Ecology and Natural Resources	Science
Agriculture	Economics	

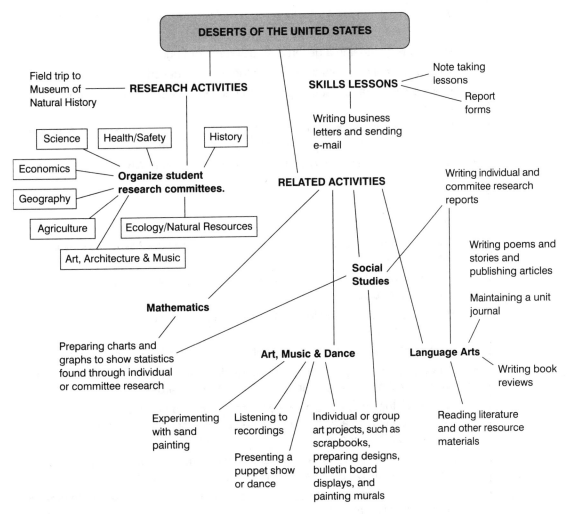

FIGURE 6.3
Diagram of a complete research-oriented thematic unit plan on "Deserts of the United States"

SAMPLE QUESTIONS TO GUIDE STUDENTS' RESEARCH

Geography

- How do we define a desert region?
- How were our deserts formed? How old are they?
- What are common features of deserts, and what defines a desert area?
- Where are deserts in the United States located?
- What are the sizes of deserts in the United States?
- Are all deserts in the United States alike in some ways? In what ways do they differ from one another?
- What is the climate like in a desert area? Is the climate the same in all of our deserts?
- How is the weather in a desert area different from our own weather?
- What seasonal changes are found in the different desert areas?
- How do climate and weather patterns in deserts affect the people who live in those areas?
- What is the population of different desert areas in the United States? What are the reasons for any variations found in population density?
- Are our deserts increasing or decreasing in population? What are some of the reasons for any changes found?

History

- Who were the first settlers in deserts of the United States? Why did they initially settle in those areas?
- How have historians and social scientists learned about early people who lived in our desert regions?
- How have artifacts found in our deserts contributed to our understanding of early civilizations?
- Which Native American tribes currently live in United States desert areas?
- How and when were the different deserts discovered by immigrants from other countries? What attracted the new settlers to those areas?
- What were the effects of discovery by new settlers on Native Americans who were living in those areas? What changes took place as a result of contacts among the different cultures?
- Do people living in desert areas live in homes similar to ours? Do they wear similar clothing? Do they have similar beliefs and customs?
- What governmental structures exist in desert areas? Are they similar to those in our own local area?

Science

- What animals and plants live in desert areas? Do the same kinds of animals and plants live in all deserts? What are the reasons for any variations found in wildlife in the different deserts?
- How are desert plants and animals adapted to desert living conditions?
- What are the effects of man-made environmental changes on animals and plants living in our deserts?
- What endangered animals and plants live in desert areas? How are they being threatened? What can be done to protect them?

Economics

- What minerals and other natural resources are found in desert areas? What effects do those resources have on desert society?
- How do people living today in desert areas earn a living?
- What products are produced in different desert areas? Is there a demand for those products?
- What objects and materials do we have in our homes that may have come from a desert in the United States?
- What types of industries are found in desert regions? Why are those industries located in a desert?
- Are any of those industries threatened by our emerging technology? In what ways?

Agriculture

- Is farming possible in desert areas? If so, what kinds of farms are found in those regions?
- What problems are faced by farmers in those areas?
- What crops are raised in deserts? What conditions would be necessary to raise other crops in the future?
- How has irrigation been used to benefit farming in a desert?

Art and Architecture

- What famous artists have lived and worked in desert areas? Why do they live there? How can their art be distinguished?
- Are there special kinds of art produced or art media used by artists who live in desert regions?
- How does the geography of desert areas affect the ways houses and other buildings are constructed?

Music

- What kinds of music and musical instruments are found in desert areas?
- What famous musicians have lived and worked in desert areas? Why did they choose to work in those areas?

Health

- What kinds of health care are available to people living in sparsely populated desert regions?
- What are the effects of desert climate on the health of people who live in those areas?
- What are the safety hazards of life in desert areas?

Language Arts

- What books have been written by authors who live in desert areas?
- What poetry has been written by people living in desert areas?
- In what ways are the books, stories, and poetry written by people in desert areas influenced by the geography, climate, and weather in those areas?
- What languages other than English are spoken in our desert areas?

POSSIBLE UNIT ACTIVITIES AND LESSONS

- Form research committees.

  There will be a committee for each area shown in the web. Each committee will have four to six children.

  After they have completed their research, the committees will be responsible for reporting their findings to the class.

  Students on each of the committees should be involved in deciding what the committee will try to investigate and how to report their findings to the class.

  Members of each committee will need to divide the work load so that each person shares in both the research and reporting.

  When forming the committees, attention will need to be given to individual student capabilities in each group. Composition of the group should be planned carefully, considering factors such as leadership, learning styles, social factors, the children's ability to share responsibilities, and their individual talents, interests, and academic capabilities.

  Encourage committee members to use a variety of reporting forms, such as displays, panel discussions, and skits.

  A "buddy" system can be developed in committees that include special needs children, who often leave the classroom during regular times devoted to research or project activities. Children who leave for special assistance programs can be paired with others in their committee groups. Their partners can review with them the committee's work during their absence.

- Provide for individual inquiry.

In addition to the subtopics being investigated by the committees, some children may have interests in subtopics that do not relate well to any committee's work.

Encourage those individuals to pursue their interests, and provide opportunities for them to report their findings to the class.

- Clarify reporting requirements for committees and individuals. Require each student to prepare a report of his/her committee research. Those who are capable of writing their reports will be asked to prepare their reports in writing. Provide the children with a form to guide their writing. The form should include information about the questions the student was researching, answers to those questions, and the sources consulted during the research phase. Ask children who write their reports to include the following information in their papers:

The committee topic and the subtopic for which the child was responsible

Questions the student used to guide his or her research

Findings (This section will need to vary in complexity according to the children's abilities. A simple list of findings, written in the student's own words, may be adequate for some children. Others will be capable of writing several paragraphs or pages.)

References (Depending on each child's abilities, the documentation format can vary from a simple list of the books and other materials used to a more sophisticated and complete documentation format.)

- Teach notetaking skills lessons.

Review and then continue the series of notetaking lessons started during the previous units.

- Teach locational skills lessons.

Ask the school librarian (or media specialist) to assist in teaching a series of lessons on locating reference materials in the media center.

- Teach lessons on writing letters and communicating with e-mail.

Many children will need to write away for information. Either give a lesson to all the children to show them an appropriate form for business letters, or assist only those who need to write letters during the unit.

Children sending e-mail will need to review the procedure for using that service.

- Offer individuals and the committees suggestions for alternative research and reporting activities.

The list will include suggestions that can be made to committees and individual children as the unit progresses. Activities address children's differing working/learning styles.

The suggestions will also include alternatives, such as making art projects and displays, or presenting puppet shows and skits, which are suitable for children with specific disabilities. Children who have difficulty preparing written reports will have alternatives, such as explaining a construction or other project or preparing a demonstration for the class.

Each student will be encouraged to use art media for a project that reflects understandings gained as a result of the desert study. Several children can elect to work together on larger projects.

Suggestions

- Use the Internet to contact a fourth grade class in one of the desert areas we are studying. Write a story describing your visit to that class.

- Compose and send a letter via e-mail to the children in a fourth grade class in a desert region asking what it is like to live in a desert region of the United States.

- Choose a story or poem on desert life from our classroom collection or from the school media center. Prepare to read it to a group of children in a kindergarten or first grade.

- Read a book from the library (either fiction or nonfiction) related to desert life. The book can be either prose or poetry. Write a review of the book that will encourage other children to read it, or prepare a story map or plot profile for fiction.

- Write a poem about one of the plants or animals that can be found in a specific desert region.

- Publish an article (using the computer) comparing living in a desert area with our area.

- Organize a panel discussion to present information your group has gained from its research.

- Prepare an oral report on an individual research project you have undertaken.

- Decide your own way of reporting the information you find through your research.

- Develop a time line to display in the classroom. Use *Timeliner,* if you would like, to prepare it. The time line needs to indicate the average rainfall each year for the past 10 or more years in a specific desert area.

- Develop a plan for an ideal desert house. Make a drawing of the plan.

- Create a graph showing some statistics, such as population changes, elevations, or average daily temperature readings, about one of the desert areas you or your committee has been studying.

- Prepare a scrapbook to show some of the information you have gained from your research.

- Draw or construct a map using other art media showing locations of different deserts in the United States.

- Draw or paint a picture showing the way an irrigation project is used to raise plants for food in a desert.

- Paint a picture or design a collage to show typical plants and/or animals found in one of the desert areas.

- Try sand painting. We can arrange with our art teacher to help those who would like to try this unique art form.

- Invite several classmates to design and paint a mural on life in the desert. The mural theme can involve animal and plant life, types of homes, typical desert scenes, or other ideas the children suggest.

- Create a three-dimensional construction showing how an irrigation project works.

- Build a model of a Native American community found in one of the desert areas studied.

- Collect pictures and articles that appear in newspapers and magazines during the unit study relating to deserts in the United States. Prepare a bulletin board display of the items collected.

- Prepare a puppet show or present a skit to the class that includes information about some of the effects new settlers had on Native Americans who were living in a desert area.

- Collect several recordings that have been written about desert living, and present the songs to the class.

- Study a Native American dance, and teach the dance to the class.

- Create a musical instrument made from materials that would be found in a desert. Demonstrate the instrument for the class.

- Work with several others to plan a classroom "museum" display of all the projects children in the class have created during the unit. Invite all children in the class to contribute their projects for the display. We can arrange to have other classes in the school visit the museum.

- Work with another person to plan a trip to one of the desert areas studied. Together, decide where to go, determine the cost, and decide the best time for such a visit.

- Maintain a journal throughout the unit to record your thoughts and feelings related to our study of deserts.

INTRODUCTORY LESSON IN THE PLANNING PHASE

Topic: Deserts of the United States

Level: Grade four

General Objective: To help children organize for their research study of their unit on deserts of the United States.

Time: 45 minutes to one hour

Behavioral Objective: After the teacher introduces the theme of the new unit and directs children's attention to research materials in the classroom, each student will begin to develop a list of the kinds of information about deserts in the United States to be found in the materials.

Procedure

1. Before beginning the unit with the children, contact the school librarian, local community children's librarian, and the art and music teachers to let them know the theme of the new unit and to invite their help during the study.

   Librarians can probably assign blocks of books or other media to the class for use during the unit. The community librarian may be able to arrange a display of materials and reserve them for the children in the class during the researching phase. The art and music teachers may be able to develop lessons related to the desert theme.

2. In addition to the social studies, science, and mathematics textbooks available in the classroom, display a sampling of library books, magazines, charts, maps, and other research materials that have been brought from the two libraries. Keep the display small so the children will be motivated to locate other materials themselves.

3. At the first class session, remind the children of the unit they have recently completed on their local region and the Atlantic Coast, and review some of the major concepts they gained from that study.

   The children should recall that coastal areas are important contributors to our inland areas. The natural harbors along the coast have served for many years as major sites for importing goods from all over the world—especially New York Harbor in the children's immediate area. Children will mention the fishing industry and will recall that there is a concentration of population along the Atlantic Coast.

4. Explain that the new unit will be a study of deserts in the United States and that it will focus on life in desert areas and ways people are affected by desert living.

5. Ask the children what they know about deserts, and construct a concept web to record their responses on the chalkboard and later transfer to a chart. (See Figure 5.7 in Chapter 5 for an example of a concept web.) The chart can be modified as the children gain new information; they may need to delete inaccuracies in their original ideas and add other concepts discovered through their studies.

6. Tell the children they will be helping to plan the study and that the first step is to skim available research materials to learn the kinds of information they will be able to find using available resources.

7. Direct the children's attention to the small classroom display of books, magazines, and other materials on deserts in the United States. Explain that these materials have been brought into the classroom for use during the unit and that additional sources will need to be located, some of which are available in the school media center.

8. Ask for three or four volunteers to go to the school library to meet with the librarian, who will assist them in locating other materials for the classroom. Have the class secretary keep a list of volunteers' names. Ask one of the volunteers to go to the library to speak to the librarian about a suitable time.

9. Ask for another five volunteers to accompany the teacher on a walk to the local public library to locate more materials on desert living. Have the class secretary keep a list of their names. Explain that the teacher will meet with them later in the day to make arrangements for their noon walk to the library.

   Permission slips can be distributed during the small group meeting. Allow several days for returning the slips when scheduling the library trip.

10. Ask the class if anyone can think of sources, other than libraries, where information about deserts in the United States might be found.

    The children will probably mention travel agencies, public television programs, computer programs and the Internet, state agencies, and chambers of commerce in desert areas.

11. Explain that over the next several days they will need to look through the research materials in the room (and those to be brought from the libraries by children) to learn the kinds of information they can expect to find about deserts in the United States. Ask students to keep a list of the kinds of information they find in the materials. Tell them that they will be asked to give their lists to the class secretary after three days. The secretary will then choose several people to help compile one list (to eliminate duplicate entries). The final list will be duplicated for the class.

12. Explain that the main point of looking through the materials at this time is simply to get an idea of what information is available. They need not read extensively, but only note and record the kinds of information they find.

13. Review with the class ways to locate information in the various materials available: using the table of contents, index, captions, boldface headings, etc.

14. Provide 20 to 25 minutes for the children to peruse materials available in the classroom. Remind them to start their lists in their notebooks.

15. As the children begin, assist them to be certain that they understand the assignment. Meet briefly with the two ad hoc groups to make arrangements for their library visits. Distribute permission slips to children who will walk to the community library at noon.

Materials

- A variety of science and social studies textbooks from several publishers, and a selection of books from the media center in the school and from the public library.

- Magazines and newspapers with relevant articles and pictures.

- Computer software, such as CD-ROM encyclopedias and special programs on the desert theme.

DESCRIPTION OF THE REMAINDER OF THE PLANNING PHASE

1. After a composite of the kinds of information included in children's available resources has been compiled, duplicated, and distributed to the class, elicit the children's help in organizing general categories for the items the new list includes. For example, *temperature, climate, rainfall,* and *wind* may all be on the list. They can be combined to form the general category—or subtopic—*weather.* Develop an outline with the children of all the subtopics, and have the class secretary copy it for duplication.

2. Duplicate and distribute the outline to each child in the class. Ask each student to list three choices of subtopics for a committee assignment on a slip of paper. Collect the requests and prepare a list of committee assignments.

   The committee assignments should be made with consideration for the social makeup, leadership, and heterogeneity of each group. It will be important to ensure that individuals work on different kinds of committees throughout the year. For example, a child should not always be assigned to the economics committee or the art committee. Final committee assignments are made by the teacher. If any important subtopic is not selected by anyone, several children can be asked if they will form that specific committee, or the teacher can assume responsibility for that area.

3. The committee assignments should then be duplicated and distributed to each child, and the first meeting of committees should be announced. Before committees meet, discuss the meaning of "committee" and how a committee should function. At the first meeting, each committee should select a chairperson and recorder, and the children should decide how they will divide the committee responsibilities among them. The recorder should be directed to write this information for the teacher. In that way, the teacher will know what each student in the class is investigating. The planning phase ends after the initial committee meetings.

DESCRIPTION OF THE RESEARCH PHASE

1. Once the work of the unit has been divided among committees, each period devoted to research should begin with a *progress report* from each committee chairperson. Any problems in locating needed information, the need for art materials for projects, and how well the group is doing on its subtopic should be shared with the class. The remainder of the period may involve a variety of activities, all happening simultaneously. For example, some children will be reading and taking notes for their research. One or two may be viewing filmstrips or using computers in a corner of the room. Several children may be working on the mural in the hall, two or three children may have signed out for the library, and others may be meeting with the art or music teacher for help with their projects.

2. Throughout the researching phase, the teacher will meet with individual children on a rotating basis to monitor progress and to provide any special help needed.

When not meeting with individuals, the teacher will be circulating among the committees and assisting children with various projects. Once the committee work is progressing, each group should be asked to decide how it would prefer to report its findings to the class. It is important to encourage variety in reporting methods. Suggestions, such as panels, demonstrations, drama, dance, displays, etc., should be given. During the researching phase, the teacher will also give a series of skills lessons in language arts on locating research, taking notes, and writing away for information using a business letter form.

3. The researching phase draws to a close as the committees complete their work. Each committee should then be scheduled to present its report to the class. It is anticipated that the committees will not all finish at the same time, so reports can be spread over a period of several days or a week at the end of the unit.

DESCRIPTION OF THE REPORTING PHASE

1. Schedule the committee reports for this phase of the unit—one or two presentations for each day.

2. Before each committee begins its presentation, remind the class about good listening habits and suggest note taking during the report so that important information will not be forgotten. Explain that the most important material from the committee's report will need to be outlined after the presentation.

3. After each committee presentation, ask the class to participate in developing an outline of the most important information they gleaned from the committee report. Assist the children with the outline, using a conventional (I., A., 1., a.) outline form and writing it on the board.

4. Have all children copy the outline in their notebooks. Explain that the outline will help them when they study for the final unit examination.

5. After all committees have reported and the children have a complete set of outlines for all committee reports recorded in their notebooks, ask committees to meet once again to prepare three or four important questions about their subtopic. Explain that the questions will be used for a review session before the final examination and that it is possible that some of their questions will be on the actual test.

   If any of the committee-generated questions are used for the exam, the teacher will edit them for clarity, grammar, and punctuation.

6. Hold a review session with the class. Have committee chairpersons read some of their questions for the class to discuss and answer. Limit questions to no more than two from any committee for the review session.

7. Administer the unit examination. Formats and questions of the examination will depend on the material presented in committee reports. A combination of multiple choice, true/false, completion, and limited-response essay formats will probably be needed.

8. Return all materials to the children: examinations, research reports (from committee research), book reports, and art projects. Hold a drawing of names of interested children to determine who will be able to take the mural home after it has been displayed for a week or two.

EVALUATION TECHNIQUES

- Use observation to note children's individual progress in organizing, sharing, and participating in committee work.
- Observe as children take notes for their research projects to determine specific skills that will need to be stressed in future note-taking lessons.
- Review all written reports to assess the progress children are making with their writing skills and in organizing their research and book reports.
- Take photographs of the children's art projects as they develop during the unit.
- Examine children's projects to determine the extent to which they reflect the concepts they have studied and to note the progress being made in using various art and construction media.
- Have each student maintain a unit portfolio that includes the following materials:

  A file of notes taken for individual research

  Samples of written work or work in progress, including letters, creative writing, and written reports

  Samples or photographs of art projects, constructions, charts or graphs, or works in progress

  A journal reflecting on the student's own work during the unit

  Records of experiments children have designed and completed

  Records or notes on any individual pupil/teacher conferences

  Unit examination

- Collect children's portfolios and add notes about each student's work habits and ability to work with others cooperatively.
- Administer a comprehensive examination at the end of the unit to evaluate the children's mastery of major concepts developed in the unit of study.

MATERIALS

- Social studies and science textbooks from a variety of publishers should be available in sufficient quantities; four to six copies of each textbook are adequate.
- Trade books from the school and public library on desert areas in the United States
- Films, filmstrips, and videotapes on deserts of the United States

- Computer software and related CD–ROM titles
- Computer technological services and consultation on the Internet for sources of information
- Brochures from travel agencies that highlight desert vacation areas
- Art materials for projects and report covers

Clearly, planning a new research-oriented thematic unit is a highly professional task involving a great deal of time, thought, and effort. Each time the same unit is used again with a new group of children, it will need to be updated and perhaps modified. New activities and research materials can be added; others found to be ineffective in the past can be eliminated from the plan.

Modifying a Research-Oriented Unit Plan for a Departmentalized School

Nearly any theme that is taught in a departmentalized intermediate or middle school curriculum can be approached from an interdisciplinary perspective. Although teachers in departmentalized schools work independently from one another much of the time, there is a growing trend toward a teaming organization in many middle schools. With or without teaching teams, it is feasible to develop a unit plan in which all teachers who work with the same group of students address a common theme for at least a part of their class time.

In the middle school, themes are more comprehensive than in the lower grades; the themes vary somewhat from school to school, depending on state and local requirements and departmental guidelines. Theme studies range considerably in grades five through eight and may include studies of the pre-Columbian period to present-day America, and social, economic, and geographic studies of the United States, Canada, Latin America, Africa, Asia, Western and Eastern Europe, the Mediterranean, and other regions. Some themes focus on our emerging nation and its governmental processes and structures.

Because the "Deserts . . ." unit has already been developed in some detail in this chapter, that same theme will be used to illustrate how a research-oriented thematic unit plan can be reorganized for instruction in a departmentalized school. The adaptation will continue to foster valuable connections among disciplines with minimal disruption to the departmental structure of the school.

Interdisciplinary units will usually summon contributions from all or most departments: science, social studies, mathematics, English, reading or language arts, health, physical education, art, and music, as well as the school nurse or nurse-teacher. Ideally, participation should be voluntary, and when plans for the unit are being prepared, input should be invited from everyone who will be involved. As an initial step, an organizational meeting can be arranged for the teachers who will participate in teaching the unit. Administrative support may be needed to help set aside a convenient time for the meeting, especially in schools without existing instructional teams.

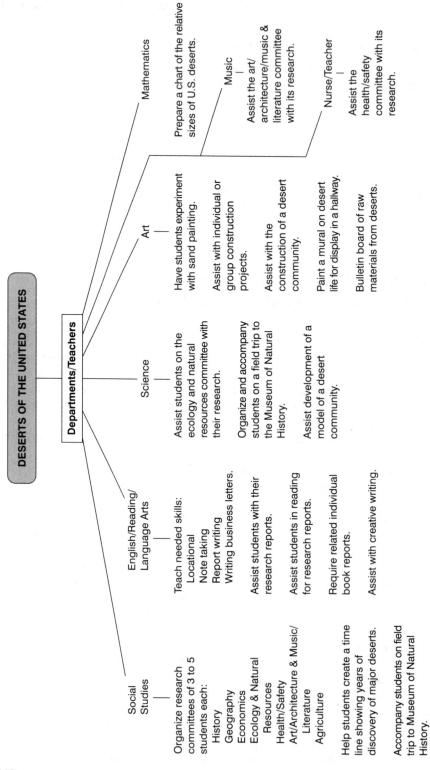

DESERTS OF THE UNITED STATES

Departments/Teachers

Social Studies

Organize research committees of 3 to 5 students each:
History
Geography
Economics
Ecology & Natural Resources
Health/Safety
Art/Architecture & Music/Literature
Agriculture

Help students create a time line showing years of discovery of major deserts.

Accompany students on field trip to Museum of Natural History.

Assist students in locating information for research reports.

English/Reading/Language Arts

Teach needed skills:
Locational
Note taking
Report writing
Writing business letters.

Assist students with their research reports.

Assist students in reading for research reports.

Require related individual book reports.

Assist with creative writing.

Science

Assist students on the ecology and natural resources committee with their research.

Organize and accompany students on a field trip to the Museum of Natural History.

Assist development of a model of a desert community.

Art

Have students experiment with sand painting.

Assist with individual or group construction projects.

Assist with the construction of a desert community.

Paint a mural on desert life for display in a hallway.

Bulletin board of raw materials from deserts.

Mathematics

Prepare a chart of the relative sizes of U.S. deserts.

Music
—
Assist the art/architecture/music & literature committee with its research.

Nurse/Teacher
—
Assist the health/safety committee with its research.

FIGURE 6.4
Plan for a research-oriented thematic unit in a departmentalized school

The basic unit plan outline for the "Deserts" theme can be used as the team decides how to organize the study. Responsibility for student committee work can be divided among several teachers according their individual specialties. The teachers need to decide where the committee work can best be organized and supervised; that is, which teacher or teachers will assume the primary responsibility for beginning the unit and assigning students to their committees. For some themes, this may be the social studies teacher; for others, the science, reading, English, language arts, or other teacher may be the most appropriate teacher to organize the student committees.

The web for a departmentalized approach to the "Deserts" unit has been redesigned to suggest each department's responsibilities. The illustration in Figure 6.4 suggests each teacher's role in the unit's development.

The main areas of responsibility have been distributed among the teachers. Each teacher will be able to operate both independently and as part of an instructional "team" in developing the unit. Most of the time, the teachers will be able to complete their part of the instructional plan separately or with minimal consultation with the other teachers. In the diagram, some collaborative efforts are indicated, such as those between the art and science teachers who will develop a plan and assist the students in constructing a model desert village. The science and social studies teachers will cooperate for the field trip. The English/reading/language arts teacher will take a central role in reinforcing the skills students will need to take notes and write their reports.

This model is only one way to organize for an interdisciplinary study in a departmentalized situation; teachers and administrators who believe the interdisciplinary approach is valuable for students in their schools will need to search for creative ways to implement it in the context of their school programs. To be viable, interdisciplinary, interdepartmental teaching will require both administrative support and collaboration among teachers. The need for system-wide support for interdisciplinary instruction will be emphasized further in Chapter 7.

References

Charbonneau, M. P., & Reider, B. E. (1995). *The integrated elementary classroom: A developmental model of education for the 21st century.* Needham Heights, MA: Allyn & Bacon.

Criteria for Selection of Class Research Topics. (1966, April 28). *Our 3 C's—Characteristic curricular concepts, 12*(12). Union Free School District No. 25, Merrick, New York.

Ellis, A. K. (1995). *Teaching and learning elementary social studies* (5th ed.). Boston: Allyn & Bacon.

Humphreys, A., Post, R., & Ellis, A. K. (1981). *Interdisciplinary methods: A thematic approach.* Santa Monica, CA: Goodyear.

Jacobs, H. (Ed.). (1989). *Interdisciplinary curriculum: Design and implementation.* Alexandria, VA: Association for Supervision and Curriculum Development.

Johnson, D. W., Johnson, R. T., & Holubec, E. J. (1994). *Cooperative learning in the classroom.* Alexandria, VA: Association for Supervision and Curriculum Development.

Kellough, R. D., & Kellough, N. G. (1996). *Middle school teaching: A guide to methods and resources* (2nd ed.). Upper Saddle River, NJ: Merrill/Prentice Hall.

Lyman, L., Foyle, H., & Azwell, T. (1993). *Cooperative learning in the elementary classroom.* Washington, DC: National Education Association.

Pappas, C. C., Kiefer, B. Z., & Levstik, L. S. (1995). *An integrated language perspective in the elementary school.* White Plains, NY: Longman.

Roberts, P. L., & Kellough, R. D. (1996). *A guide for developing an interdisciplinary thematic unit.* Upper Saddle River, NJ: Merrill/Prentice Hall.

Rottier, J., & Ogan, B. J. (1991). *Cooperative learning in middle-level schools.* Washington, DC: National Education Association.

Suggested Readings

Davies, I. K. (1976). *Objectives in curriculum design.* London: McGraw-Hill.

Dembo, M. H. (1988). *Applying educational psychology in the classroom* (3rd ed.). New York: Longman.

Dick, W., & Carey, L. (1978). *The systematic design of instruction.* Glenview, IL: Scott, Foresman.

Gronlund, N. E. (1985). *Stating objectives for classroom instruction* (3rd ed.). New York: Macmillan.

Grosvenor, L. (1993). *Student portfolios.* Washington, DC: National Education Association.

Kibler, R. J., Cegala, D. J., Barker, L. L., & Miles, D. T. (1974). *Objectives for instruction and evaluation* (2nd ed.). Boston: Allyn & Bacon.

Mager, R. (1984). *Preparing instructional objectives* (Rev. 2nd ed.). Belmont, CA: Lake Management & Training.

Mason, E. (1972). *Collaborative learning.* New York: Agathon Press.

Messick, R. G., & Reynolds, K. E. (1992). *Middle level curriculum in action.* White Plains, NY: Longman.

O'Neil, J. (1993, September). The promise of portfolios. *Update, 35*(7), 1–5.

Reigeluth, C. M. (1987). *Instructional theories in action: Lessons illustrating selected theories and models.* Hillsdale, NJ: Erlbaum.

Wadsworth, B. J. (1978). *Piaget for the classroom teacher.* New York: Longman.

Weinland, T. P., & Protheroe, D. W. (1973). *Social science projects you can do.* Upper Saddle River, NJ: Prentice Hall.

7

Interdisciplinary Instruction and the Change Process

The final chapter:

- *Considers the process of change involved in moving toward an interdisciplinary program.*
- *Discusses an important question about the change process: "What kinds of support do teachers need from their school systems in order to develop an interdisciplinary instructional program?"*
- *Summarizes main points presented in support of the interdisciplinary method and lists its major values for students.*

Moving Toward an Interdisciplinary Program

The thrust toward interdisciplinary instruction is not the only challenge confronting teachers and schools today.

> Teachers are told that they have to set higher standards for all students, eliminate tracking, tailor lessons to kids' individual needs (including those with various disabilities), adopt small-group and cooperative learning techniques, design interdisciplinary and multicultural curricula, work in teams with other teachers, promote "critical" and "creative" thinking instead of rote learning, attend to children's social and emotional needs, rely on "performance assessment" instead of multiple-choice tests, get with the latest technology, encourage active learning in "real-life" contexts, use fewer textbooks, and, on top of everything else, become "agents of change" in their schools. (Miller, 1995, p. 2)

Recommendations come from many sources, both from within and outside the teaching profession. Sometimes teachers have inspired others to make changes. At times, teachers have written about methods they have developed or which have grown from their personal teaching experiences and observations. Well-known teacher-authors of the past include Ashton-Warner (1963), Barth (1972), Channon (1970), Dennison (1969), Kohl (1967), and Richardson (1964). Some advocated more humanistic approaches in educating children (Hentoff, 1966; Holt, 1964, 1967, 1969). Occasionally, educational critics have pressed for radical school reforms (Gross & Gross, 1969; Kozol, 1975; Pines, 1967; Postman & Weingartner, 1969; Silberman, 1970).

Why Teachers Are Slow to Change Methods

Each year, new voices add their criticisms and recommend modifications to our educational programs, yet most of the changes they suggest tend to evolve very slowly if at all in actual practice.

A number of years ago, Leonard (1968) cited several major reasons for the reluctance of teachers to act rapidly on any changes that are recommended. Leonard's thinking is logical, and it is applicable today.

> A certain caution in educational matters is quite understandable. A school child is far more complex, embodying far more variables, than NASA's entire satellite communications network. Baffled by this complexity and inhibited by a reluctance to "experiment" with children's lives, educators feel justified in clinging to methods that have been developed, hit or miss, over the centuries—even when they are shown to be inefficient. (p. 214)

Leonard's reasoning makes the cautious acceptance of changes in teaching understandable, especially if the changes suggested are very new or if there is a lack of sufficient evidence from research to support their effectiveness. Reluctance about the interdisciplinary method, however, is not quite as easy to understand, mainly because the method is not new or revolutionary; it has already been used by teachers for many years. An integrated approach to curriculum is no longer considered to be *experimental* by most educators.

We have very little information, however, about the success of the interdisciplinary method from the schools where it has actually been tried. The lack of documented evidence and information from the practical experiences of others may well contribute to teachers' reluctance to try it.

Research and the Interdisciplinary Method

Recently, teachers have been presented with materials that can help promote the interdisciplinary approach. For example, "Cross Subject Teaching" (1993), a videotape presentation, attempts to demonstrate its benefits in schools where it is actually being tried. The video shows ways in which music has been integrated into other disciplines across a school curriculum in an Appalachian school.

Although formal reports from schools have been relatively rare in the past, in 1968, Roland Chatterton, an administrator in a suburban community on Long Island, New York, produced and directed two unique documentary films illustrating a *multidisciplinary*, unit-centered instructional program that had been developed by the teachers in his schools (Chatterton, 1968). Each film shows a master teacher, Joyce Schoenberger Mills, guiding a group of fifth-grade children through two research-oriented thematic units. Special area teacher/consultants in art, music, library/media, and health are observed assisting the classroom teacher and children with their research, projects, and presentations.

The Chatterton films follow the children and teachers engaged in various lessons and activities throughout the five to six weeks it took to complete their interdisciplinary unit. The presentation intentionally leaves the value of the interdisciplinary approach for the viewer to decide. Although the documentaries are both inspiring and convincing, and the method's positive results are implied by the film director, neither film reports any research that might have been undertaken by the school system to document its values. Viewers are, therefore, left to wonder if any objective evidence had been collected to indicate that the approach had in fact been more effective than other methods. (Some colleges and universities have copies of these unusual films, but unfortunately, the film company that produced them no longer exists.)

Until there are more serious research studies and formal reports on the method from the schools in which it is tried, movement toward interdisciplinary instruction will probably continue slowly, and teachers may continue to be reluctant about trying the method in their own classes.

The Need for System Support

The sluggish pace of change toward interdisciplinary instruction is especially disturbing when its potential values for students, which were reviewed in the first chapter of this book, are considered. Perhaps as more state education departments add their support and recommend the method, the present situation will change, and more school systems will introduce the method, undertake studies of its value, and issue formal reports of their experiences. Any change will still take time and commitment, not only from individual teachers but from school systems as well.

Effecting Curricular Change

A number of important factors are involved in making any such system-wide curricular change. Initially, an orderly process for instituting any change must be outlined. It is not necessary to invent a completely new procedure because a number of excellent models already exist. For example, Wiles and Bondi (1989) provide insights and suggestions for educators contemplating curricular revisions. The writers offer a valuable outline of the tasks involved and leadership requirements for the change process. Oliva (1988) explains several alternative models useful in making curricular changes; he also proposes one of his own that appears to be well suited for the shift from traditional to interdisciplinary programs.

The Oliva model begins with an outline of program aims and philosophical and psychological principles upon which the new curriculum is to be based. Other steps involve analysis of community and student needs, and stating goals and objectives. Listing steps toward implementation of the new program and evaluation procedures complete the process. Oliva's model is flexible, and his statement, "the faculty may develop school-wide, interdisciplinary programs that act across areas of specialization," indicates that the model is applicable for introducing interdisciplinary instruction in departmentalized middle schools (p. 176).

Earlier, Frymier (1973) had outlined a six-phase process for curricular change in schools. Even though Frymier was talking to educators of the 1970s, the same phases—or steps—he proposed can still be useful for school systems intending to move toward an interdisciplinary curricular program. Frymier explains his six-phase plan as follows:

. . . awareness of the need for change; conceptualizing a range of alternatives; exploration and consideration of the alternatives; commitment and institutionalization of the proposal for change; preparation of staff; implementation, evaluation, and modification of the change. (p. 289)

Adequate planning, staff preparation, and system-wide support are strongly implied in this list. In fact, preparation and support may well be the key factors to success in the interdisciplinary curricular change process. Any methodological change can place heavy demands on a school system; this is especially true of the interdisciplinary approach because both inservice preparation and new instructional materials may be needed.

Teacher and Classroom Needs

Certainly, if any progress toward interdisciplinary instruction is to last, teachers will need preparation for their new role and support throughout the transitional period. The teachers who will use the new approach should be consulted and involved in the change process from the outset; whenever teachers are not included in the initial decision-making steps or administrative support is weak, the movement toward an interdisciplinary program—or any other instructional modification—is unlikely to be successful. Of course, the teaching staff should also be involved in selecting the themes they will be teaching for their interdisciplinary units, and they should be given time to share the designs of their unit plans with one another. Preferably, opportunities should be scheduled for those tasks during the school day.

In addition to support from the school system, teachers need to have opportunities to form networks where they can work together to effect the changes they believe are appropriate for the students in their schools (Miller, 1995). Again, such collaboration cannot take place without adequate time and administrative backing.

The teaching staff may also need new materials. Both the kind and the quantity of instructional materials will change with interdisciplinary methods. For example, instead of a textbook from one publisher for each child in a class, classrooms need a collection of five or six copies of social studies and science textbooks from each of several different publishers so that students will have access to more than one viewpoint as they research their unit themes. Purchasing the new materials will, of course, involve additional funding.

All classrooms should be equipped with computers and a supply of computer software programs. Teachers need to have access to software catalogs from various suppliers in order to study new programs that are being produced continuously. Computer networking opportunities should be carefully explored and added if found to be valuable and feasible; Carlitz and Lentz (1995) offer an especially helpful list and discussion of the standards educators should consider when making decisions about these networking opportunities.

Teachers also need a supply of trade books on unit themes; some will be kept in individual classrooms, others can be centrally located in the school library or media center. The media center should house enough books, magazines, videotape programs, films, filmstrips, and other resource materials so that students from different classrooms who are studying similar themes at the same time will have an adequate, up-to-date supply of reference materials.

Clearly, any movement toward the interdisciplinary approach will require considerable time and effort from the teaching staff and support from the administration in the school system. It is also likely that additional funding will be needed to effect the change.

Conclusion

Interest in interdisciplinary instruction has increased, and the demand for information about it is growing. This book has provided preservice and inservice teachers and administrators with an introduction to the theoretical and developmental foundations of interdisciplinary instruction, and offered practical suggestions for planning two types of interdisciplinary instructional units.

Features of the interdisciplinary method that distinguish it from other educational approaches have been discussed. One of its primary characteristics is that interdisciplinary instruction involves a unique, thematic or research-oriented thematic, unit-centered approach to the study of social topics. A second feature is that teachers who use the method are always concerned about helping students develop the processes as well as the skills they will need in order to learn throughout life. In particular, students gain experience with the research process, the scientific method, and ways of knowing inherent in different disciplinary areas as they investigate their unit themes. Students also find many natural opportunities to practice their academic skills as they study a theme and prepare reports of their findings.

Points in Support of Interdisciplinary Instruction

Interdisciplinary instruction at the elementary and middle school levels can be supported in several ways. First, holistic studies of themes help students to note the interrelationships among the disciplines and to realize that they often need to apply the skills from more than one discipline whenever they study a social topic or need to solve a problem in real life.

Second, the interdisciplinary method exposes students to a greater variety of resources than traditional, disciplinary approaches, which use a single textbook as a resource. Therefore, teachers are better able to ensure that students are provided with a wide variety of materials that offer a more rounded, less biased viewpoint, especially in the social studies and science disciplines.

A third reason for interdisciplinary instruction is that, when compared with more conventional approaches to education, it may be more suitable for students with special needs because it permits greater flexibility in scheduling, and it supports the use of alternative research methods and reporting techniques. These are attributes that are especially important for and appreciated by students who need extra time and help in order to learn while they participate along with their peers in regular classrooms.

Teachers who use interdisciplinary instruction find it to be professionally demanding. To be successful, they need to become secure in the unit planning process and in managing their classrooms. To assist those who are unfamiliar with the unit planning process, both thematic and research-oriented thematic units have been explained in this book. Step-by-step instructions, along with examples, have been given to help teachers begin the unit planning process.

Skills Required of Teachers

This book has also emphasized that interdisciplinary teachers need to have an extensive fund of general knowledge. They must also be capable of applying their understandings of child development, and must consider the fundamental learning theories and principles when planning their units. Individual differences in students also require teachers to study the diverse learning styles of students and to adapt instruction to the ways students can learn best.

Benefits to Children

The discussion in this book has also attempted to emphasize what is most beneficial to students who are taught to use an interdisciplinary approach to their studies. Students are encouraged to develop the higher-level thinking skills and to recognize that several disciplines and subcategories within the disciplines usually have to be examined when investigating a theme. They discover that their inquiries are often *open-ended* and *continuing* rather than *finished* or *complete*. Interdisciplinary units always provide students with specific, individual responsibilities, and students work at their own ability levels. Whenever they work with others in cooperative research groups or serve on committees, they learn how to work together and share responsibilities. Finally, using an interdisciplinary approach, students discover a great variety of resources that can be consulted for the themes they study, not only while they are in school but as they continue to learn throughout their lives.

References

Ashton-Warner, S. (1963). *Teacher.* New York: Simon & Schuster.

Barth, R. S. (1972). *Open education and the American school.* New York: Agathon Press.

Carlitz, R. D., & Lentz, M. (1995, April). Standards for school networking. *T.H.E. Journal*, 22(9), 71–74.

Channon, G. (1970). *Homework.* New York: Outerbridge & Dienstfrey.

Chatterton, R. (1968). *The multidisciplinary teaching of class research topics.* Merrick School District No. 25. Merrick, New York.

Cross subject teaching. (1993). Episode No. 4, NEA Professional Library. West Haven, CT: National Education Association.

Dennison, G. (1969). *The lives of children: The story of the first street school.* New York: Random House.

Frymier, J. R. (1973). *A school for tomorrow.* Berkeley, CA: McCutchan.

Gross, B., & Gross, R. (1969). *Radical school reform.* New York: Simon & Schuster.

Hentoff, N. (1966). *Our children are dying.* New York: Pitman.

Holt, J. (1964). *How children fail.* New York: Delta.

Holt, J. (1967). *How children learn.* New York: Pitman.

Holt, J. (1969). *The underachieving school.* New York: Pitman.

Kohl, H. (1967). *36 children.* New York: Signet.

Kozol, J. (1975). *The night is dark and I am far from home.* Boston: Houghton Mifflin.

Leonard, G. B. (1968). *Education and ecstasy.* New York: Delacorte Press.

Miller, E. (1995, January/February). The old model of staff development survives in a world where everything else has changed. *The Harvard Education Letter, 11*(1), 1–3.

Oliva, P. F. (1988). *Developing the curriculum* (2nd ed.). Glenview, IL: Scott, Foresman.

Pines, M. (1966). *Revolution in learning: The years from birth to six.* New York: Harper & Row.

Postman, N., & Weingartner, C. (1969). *Teaching as a subversive activity.* New York: Delacorte Press.

Richardson, E. S. (1964). *In the early world.* New York: Pantheon Books.

Silberman, C. E. (1970). *Crisis in the classroom: The remaking of American education.* New York: Random House.

Wiles, J., & Bondi, J. (1989). *Curriculum development: A guide to practice* (3rd ed.). Upper Saddle River, NJ: Merrill/Prentice Hall.

Suggested Readings

Fraser, H. W. (1985). Microcomputers in schools. *The Educational Forum, 50*(1), 87–100.

Herndon, J. (1968). *The way it spozed to be.* New York: Simon & Schuster.

Hertzberg, A., & Stone, E. F. (1971). *Schools are for children: An American approach to the open classroom.* New York: Schocken Books.

Knirk, F. G., & Gustafson, K. L. (1986). *Instructional technology: A systematic approach to education.* New York: Holt, Rinehart & Winston.

Kohl, H. R. (1969). *The open classroom: A practical guide to a new way of teaching.* New York: New York Review/Random.

Parker, R., & Parker, B. J. A historical perspective on school reform. *The Educational Forum, 59*(3), 278–87.

Peterson, D. (Ed.). (1984). *Intelligent schoolhouse: Readings on computers and learning.* Reston, VA: Reston.

Postman, N., & Weingartner, C. (1973). *The school book.* New York: Delacorte Press.

Sample Thematic Unit Plan Designs

The web for an interdisciplinary unit plan may be designed in a number of different ways. The purpose of the sample web designs in this appendix (Figures A.1 through A.14) is simply to show several designs that differ stylistically from one another. Because the webs vary in detail, number of ideas, and overall quality, the samples are not intended to be exemplary, but are only to show several alternative ways to construct them. The essential elements are included in each of the designs: a central theme, some of the related disciplines that will be employed to explore the theme, and brief statements or phrases to remind the planner later about the ideas he or she had in mind for related lessons and activities. Eleven of the samples were prepared by undergraduate students in teacher education who were just beginning their study of interdisciplinary unit planning.

Each sample is the result of the initial brainstorming step, described in Chapters 5 and 6, followed when planning the unit. As explained in this book, interdisciplinary webs should be designed mainly to serve as a reminder to the teacher of the kinds of activities and lessons that may be included in the unit when it is actually taught. Therefore, the webs do not give sufficient detailed information about learning options, materials, processes, or content the unit will include. In a thematic unit plan, those details are provided in the *Descriptions of Lessons and Activities* section; in a research-oriented thematic unit plan, details are included under a list of *Possible Research Committees, Sample Questions to Guide Students' Research,* and *Possible Unit Activities and Lessons*. Although a web can provide more detail, to do so usually creates a design that is overcrowded and difficult to read.

The samples indicate only a general grade level designation because it is always possible to adapt the designs for more than one grade level by adding or substituting lessons and activities. Designs for intermediate and middle school levels can be converted to become research-oriented thematic plans by adding information about student committees. The decision about the most appropriate grade placement for any theme will always depend on the students' developmental levels, their academic capabilities, the materials available for student inquiry, and local and statewide curriculum goals.

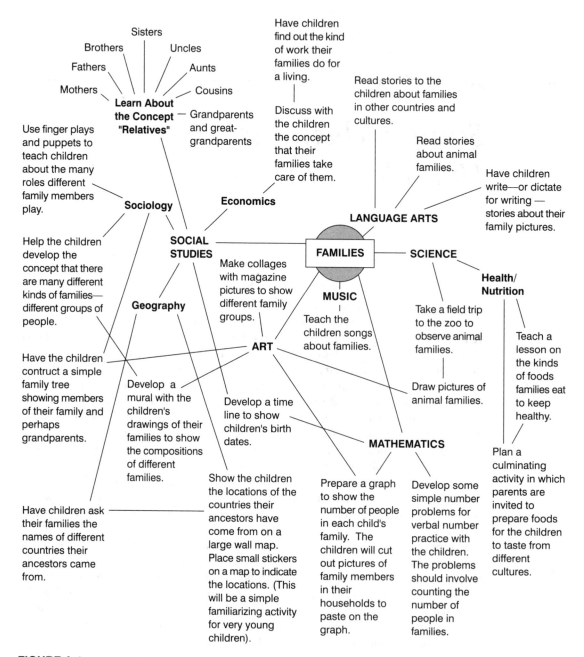

FIGURE A.1
A design for a thematic unit plan on "Families" (kindergarten and other primary grade levels)

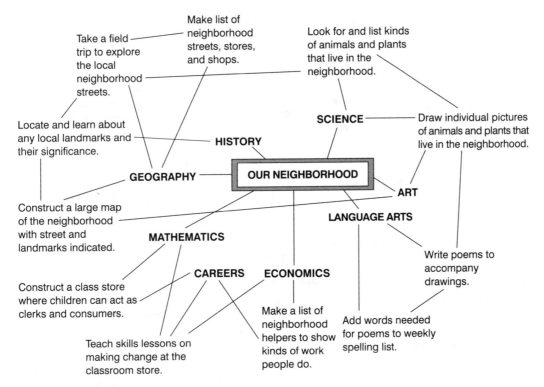

FIGURE A.2

A design for a thematic unit plan on "Our Neighborhood" (primary)

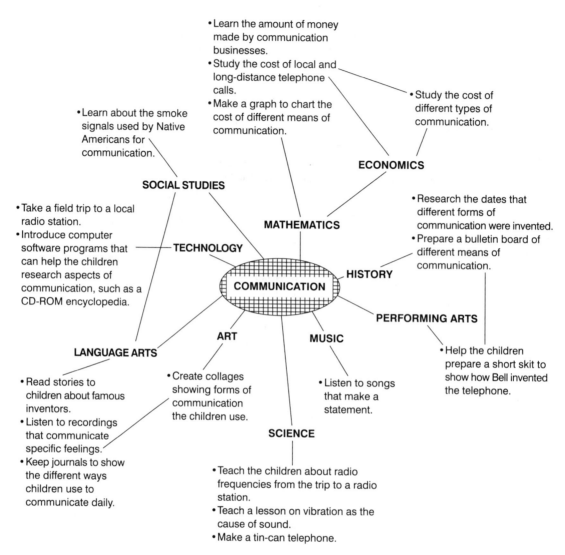

FIGURE A.3
A design for a thematic unit plan on "Communication" (intermediate)

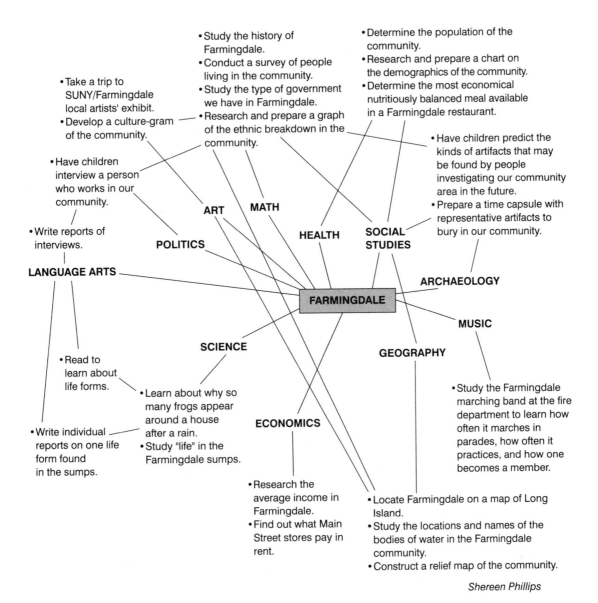

FIGURE A.4
A design for a thematic unit plan on "Farmingdale" (intermediate)

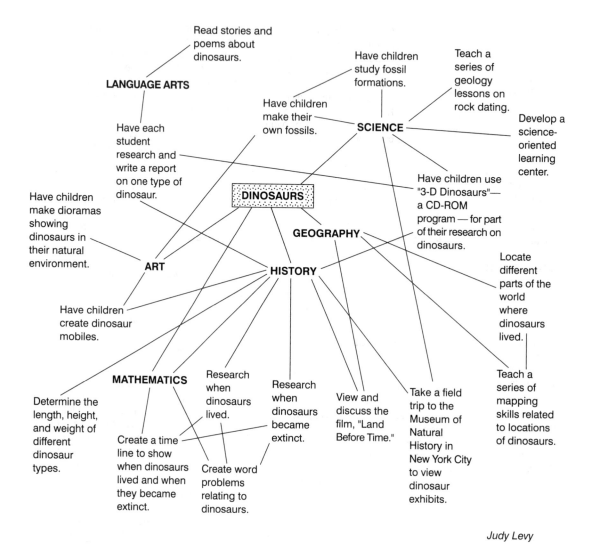

Read stories and poems about dinosaurs.

LANGUAGE ARTS

Have each student research and write a report on one type of dinosaur.

Have children study fossil formations.

Teach a series of geology lessons on rock dating.

Have children make their own fossils.

SCIENCE

Develop a science-oriented learning center.

Have children make dioramas showing dinosaurs in their natural environment.

DINOSAURS

Have children use "3-D Dinosaurs"—a CD-ROM program — for part of their research on dinosaurs.

GEOGRAPHY

ART

HISTORY

Locate different parts of the world where dinosaurs lived.

Have children create dinosaur mobiles.

MATHEMATICS

Research when dinosaurs lived.

Research when dinosaurs became extinct.

View and discuss the film, "Land Before Time."

Take a field trip to the Museum of Natural History in New York City to view dinosaur exhibits.

Teach a series of mapping skills related to locations of dinosaurs.

Determine the length, height, and weight of different dinosaur types.

Create a time line to show when dinosaurs lived and when they became extinct.

Create word problems relating to dinosaurs.

Judy Levy

FIGURE A.5
A design for a thematic unit plan on "Dinosaurs" (intermediate)

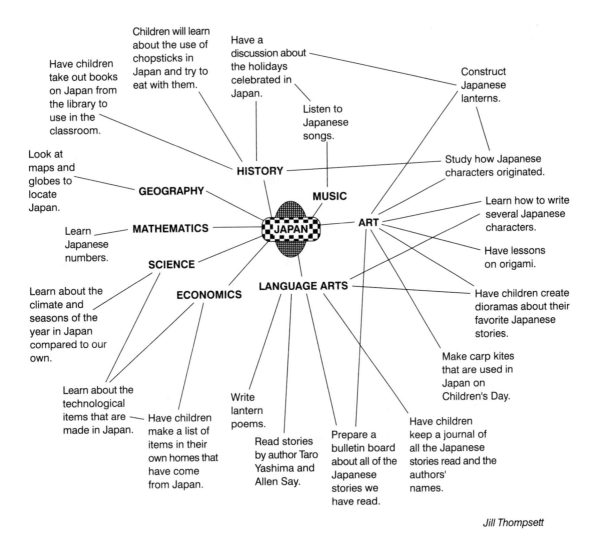

Have children take out books on Japan from the library to use in the classroom.

Children will learn about the use of chopsticks in Japan and try to eat with them.

Have a discussion about the holidays celebrated in Japan.

Construct Japanese lanterns.

Listen to Japanese songs.

Look at maps and globes to locate Japan.

Study how Japanese characters originated.

GEOGRAPHY

HISTORY

MUSIC

Learn Japanese numbers.

MATHEMATICS

JAPAN

ART

Learn how to write several Japanese characters.

Have lessons on origami.

SCIENCE

Learn about the climate and seasons of the year in Japan compared to our own.

ECONOMICS

LANGUAGE ARTS

Have children create dioramas about their favorite Japanese stories.

Make carp kites that are used in Japan on Children's Day.

Learn about the technological items that are made in Japan.

Have children make a list of items in their own homes that have come from Japan.

Write lantern poems.

Read stories by author Taro Yashima and Allen Say.

Prepare a bulletin board about all of the Japanese stories we have read.

Have children keep a journal of all the Japanese stories read and the authors' names.

Jill Thompsett

FIGURE A.6
A design for a thematic unit plan on "Japan" (intermediate)

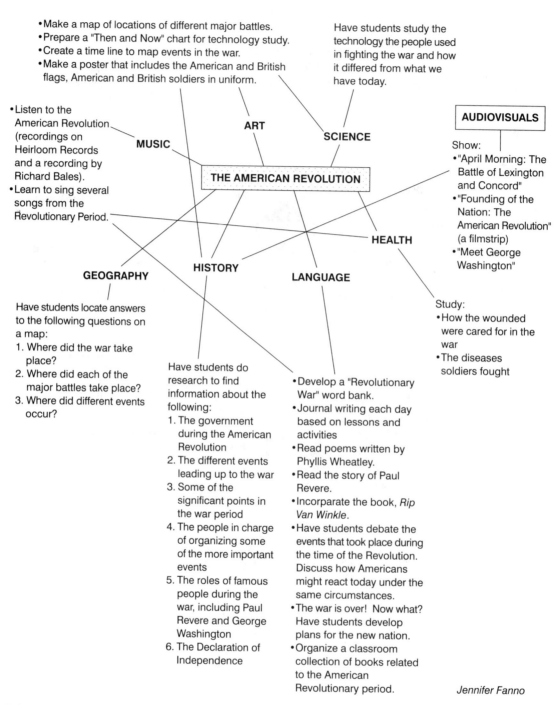

FIGURE A.7
A design for a thematic unit plan on "The American Revolution" (intermediate or above)

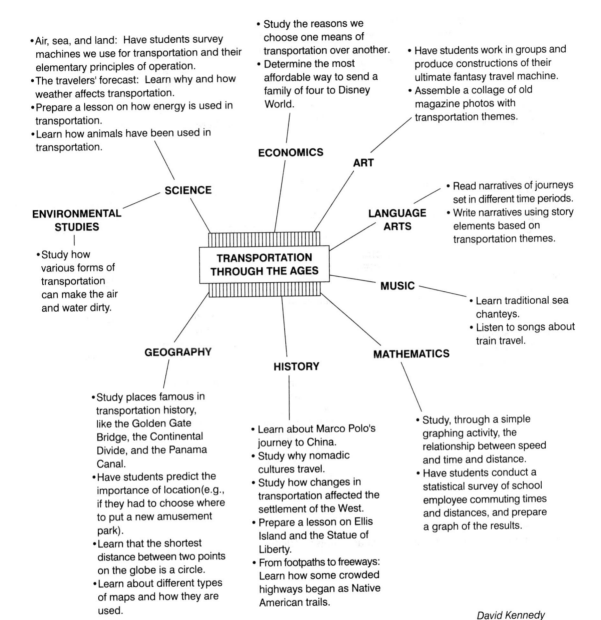

• Air, sea, and land: Have students survey machines we use for transportation and their elementary principles of operation.
• The travelers' forecast: Learn why and how weather affects transportation.
• Prepare a lesson on how energy is used in transportation.
• Learn how animals have been used in transportation.

• Study the reasons we choose one means of transportation over another.
• Determine the most affordable way to send a family of four to Disney World.

• Have students work in groups and produce constructions of their ultimate fantasy travel machine.
• Assemble a collage of old magazine photos with transportation themes.

ECONOMICS

ART

SCIENCE

LANGUAGE ARTS

• Read narratives of journeys set in different time periods.
• Write narratives using story elements based on transportation themes.

ENVIRONMENTAL STUDIES

• Study how various forms of transportation can make the air and water dirty.

TRANSPORTATION THROUGH THE AGES

MUSIC

• Learn traditional sea chanteys.
• Listen to songs about train travel.

GEOGRAPHY

HISTORY

MATHEMATICS

• Study places famous in transportation history, like the Golden Gate Bridge, the Continental Divide, and the Panama Canal.
• Have students predict the importance of location(e.g., if they had to choose where to put a new amusement park).
• Learn that the shortest distance between two points on the globe is a circle.
• Learn about different types of maps and how they are used.

• Learn about Marco Polo's journey to China.
• Study why nomadic cultures travel.
• Study how changes in transportation affected the settlement of the West.
• Prepare a lesson on Ellis Island and the Statue of Liberty.
• From footpaths to freeways: Learn how some crowded highways began as Native American trails.

• Study, through a simple graphing activity, the relationship between speed and time and distance.
• Have students conduct a statistical survey of school employee commuting times and distances, and prepare a graph of the results.

David Kennedy

FIGURE A.8
A design for a thematic unit plan on "Transportation Through the Ages" (intermediate)

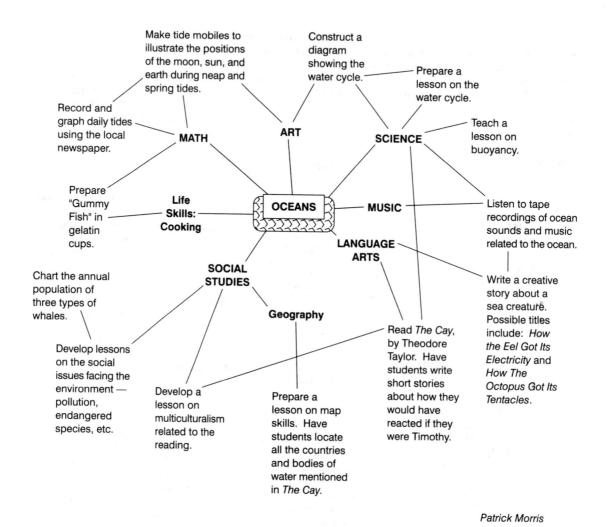

Make tide mobiles to illustrate the positions of the moon, sun, and earth during neap and spring tides.

Construct a diagram showing the water cycle.

Prepare a lesson on the water cycle.

Record and graph daily tides using the local newspaper.

MATH

ART

SCIENCE

Teach a lesson on buoyancy.

Prepare "Gummy Fish" in gelatin cups.

Life Skills: Cooking

OCEANS

MUSIC

Listen to tape recordings of ocean sounds and music related to the ocean.

LANGUAGE ARTS

Chart the annual population of three types of whales.

SOCIAL STUDIES

Write a creative story about a sea creature. Possible titles include: *How the Eel Got Its Electricity* and *How The Octopus Got Its Tentacles*.

Geography

Develop lessons on the social issues facing the environment — pollution, endangered species, etc.

Develop a lesson on multiculturalism related to the reading.

Prepare a lesson on map skills. Have students locate all the countries and bodies of water mentioned in *The Cay*.

Read *The Cay*, by Theodore Taylor. Have students write short stories about how they would have reacted if they were Timothy.

Patrick Morris

FIGURE A.9
A design for a thematic unit plan on "Oceans" (intermediate or above)

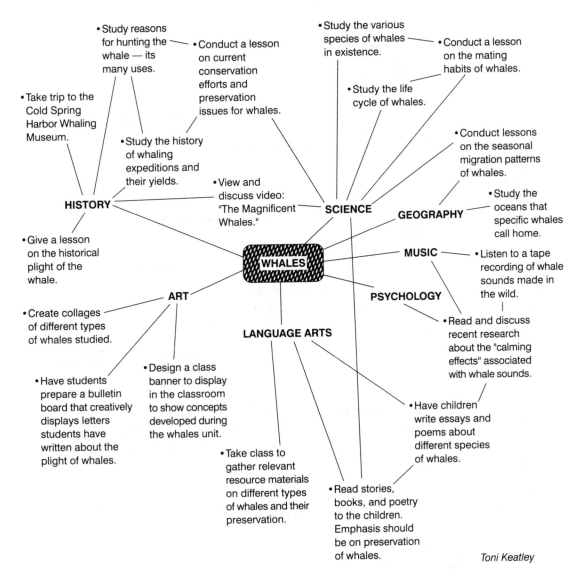

FIGURE A.10
A design for a thematic unit plan on "Whales" (intermediate)

Cooking: Try recipes with ingredients from the rain forest.

Teach measurements needed for following recipes.

Listen to tape recordings of sounds in a rain forest.

Make a graph showing amounts of rain recorded in the rain forest areas.

HEALTH/NUTRITION

Research native groups of people found in rain forest areas.

MUSIC

MATHEMATICS

Give lessons on map reading.

HISTORY

GEOGRAPHY

Locate rain forests on maps.

Prepare a bulletin board display of plants and animals found in a rain forest.

ART

RAIN FORESTS

Give a lesson on the natural layers in the rain forest.

Vocabulary: Develop a list of key words involving the study of rain forests. Add the list to regular spelling lists.

LANGUAGE ARTS

Research ways to save and preserve rain forest areas.

SCIENCE

Teach a lesson on letter writing.

Write stories about the ways people in a rain forest live.

Prepare a terrarium that simulates the climate of a rain forest.

View and discuss a film on the importance of the rain forest.

Teach a series of lessons on deforestation.

Study different plants and animals found in a rain forest.

Read stories about rain forests.

*Ann Brancale &
Katina Paulsen*

FIGURE A.11
A design for a thematic unit plan on "Rain Forests" (intermediate or above)

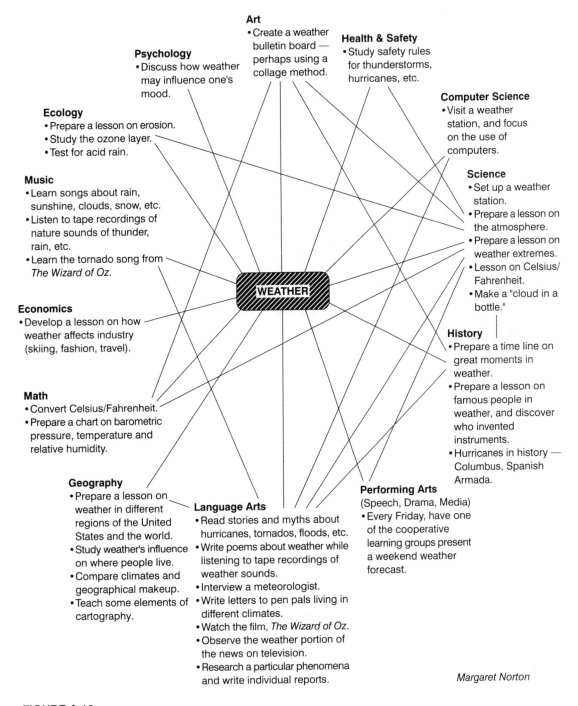

Art
• Create a weather bulletin board — perhaps using a collage method.

Psychology
• Discuss how weather may influence one's mood.

Health & Safety
• Study safety rules for thunderstorms, hurricanes, etc.

Computer Science
• Visit a weather station, and focus on the use of computers.

Ecology
• Prepare a lesson on erosion.
• Study the ozone layer.
• Test for acid rain.

Science
• Set up a weather station.
• Prepare a lesson on the atmosphere.
• Prepare a lesson on weather extremes.
• Lesson on Celsius/Fahrenheit.
• Make a "cloud in a bottle."

Music
• Learn songs about rain, sunshine, clouds, snow, etc.
• Listen to tape recordings of nature sounds of thunder, rain, etc.
• Learn the tornado song from *The Wizard of Oz.*

WEATHER

History
• Prepare a time line on great moments in weather.
• Prepare a lesson on famous people in weather, and discover who invented instruments.
• Hurricanes in history — Columbus, Spanish Armada.

Economics
• Develop a lesson on how weather affects industry (skiing, fashion, travel).

Math
• Convert Celsius/Fahrenheit.
• Prepare a chart on barometric pressure, temperature and relative humidity.

Geography
• Prepare a lesson on weather in different regions of the United States and the world.
• Study weather's influence on where people live.
• Compare climates and geographical makeup.
• Teach some elements of cartography.

Language Arts
• Read stories and myths about hurricanes, tornados, floods, etc.
• Write poems about weather while listening to tape recordings of weather sounds.
• Interview a meteorologist.
• Write letters to pen pals living in different climates.
• Watch the film, *The Wizard of Oz.*
• Observe the weather portion of the news on television.
• Research a particular phenomena and write individual reports.

Performing Arts
(Speech, Drama, Media)
• Every Friday, have one of the cooperative learning groups present a weekend weather forecast.

Margaret Norton

FIGURE A.12
A design for a thematic unit plan on "Weather" (intermediate or above)

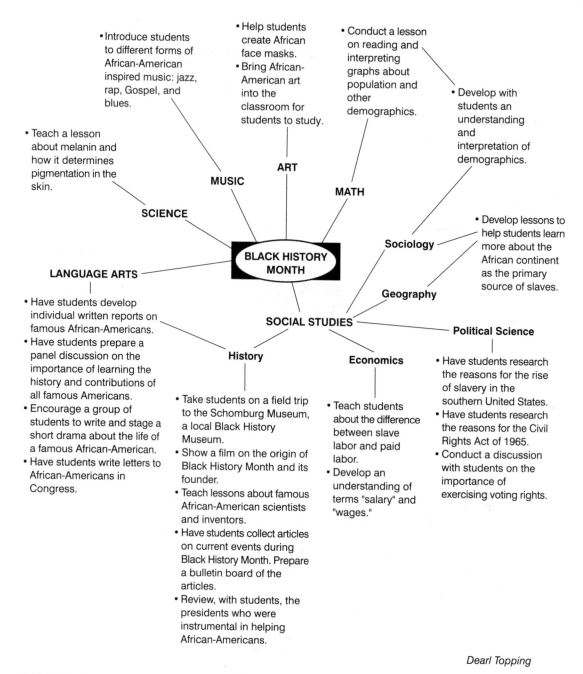

• Introduce students to different forms of African-American inspired music: jazz, rap, Gospel, and blues.

• Help students create African face masks.
• Bring African-American art into the classroom for students to study.

• Conduct a lesson on reading and interpreting graphs about population and other demographics.

• Develop with students an understanding and interpretation of demographics.

• Teach a lesson about melanin and how it determines pigmentation in the skin.

MUSIC

ART

SCIENCE

MATH

BLACK HISTORY MONTH

Sociology

• Develop lessons to help students learn more about the African continent as the primary source of slaves.

LANGUAGE ARTS

Geography

• Have students develop individual written reports on famous African-Americans.
• Have students prepare a panel discussion on the importance of learning the history and contributions of all famous Americans.
• Encourage a group of students to write and stage a short drama about the life of a famous African-American.
• Have students write letters to African-Americans in Congress.

SOCIAL STUDIES

Political Science

History

Economics

• Have students research the reasons for the rise of slavery in the southern United States.
• Have students research the reasons for the Civil Rights Act of 1965.
• Conduct a discussion with students on the importance of exercising voting rights.

• Take students on a field trip to the Schomburg Museum, a local Black History Museum.
• Show a film on the origin of Black History Month and its founder.
• Teach lessons about famous African-American scientists and inventors.
• Have students collect articles on current events during Black History Month. Prepare a bulletin board of the articles.
• Review, with students, the presidents who were instrumental in helping African-Americans.

• Teach students about the difference between slave labor and paid labor.
• Develop an understanding of terms "salary" and "wages."

Dearl Topping

FIGURE A.13
A design for a thematic unit plan on "Black History Month" (intermediate or above)

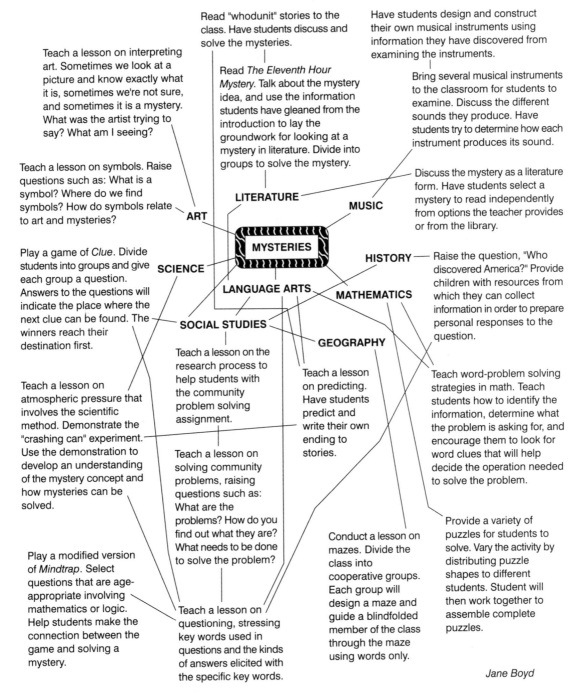

Teach a lesson on interpreting art. Sometimes we look at a picture and know exactly what it is, sometimes we're not sure, and sometimes it is a mystery. What was the artist trying to say? What am I seeing?

Teach a lesson on symbols. Raise questions such as: What is a symbol? Where do we find symbols? How do symbols relate to art and mysteries?

Play a game of *Clue*. Divide students into groups and give each group a question. Answers to the questions will indicate the place where the next clue can be found. The winners reach their destination first.

Teach a lesson on atmospheric pressure that involves the scientific method. Demonstrate the "crashing can" experiment. Use the demonstration to develop an understanding of the mystery concept and how mysteries can be solved.

Play a modified version of *Mindtrap*. Select questions that are age-appropriate involving mathematics or logic. Help students make the connection between the game and solving a mystery.

Read "whodunit" stories to the class. Have students discuss and solve the mysteries.

Read *The Eleventh Hour Mystery*. Talk about the mystery idea, and use the information students have gleaned from the introduction to lay the groundwork for looking at a mystery in literature. Divide into groups to solve the mystery.

Have students design and construct their own musical instruments using information they have discovered from examining the instruments.

Bring several musical instruments to the classroom for students to examine. Discuss the different sounds they produce. Have students try to determine how each instrument produces its sound.

Discuss the mystery as a literature form. Have students select a mystery to read independently from options the teacher provides or from the library.

LITERATURE

MUSIC

ART

MYSTERIES

SCIENCE

HISTORY

LANGUAGE ARTS

MATHEMATICS

SOCIAL STUDIES

GEOGRAPHY

Raise the question, "Who discovered America?" Provide children with resources from which they can collect information in order to prepare personal responses to the question.

Teach a lesson on the research process to help students with the community problem solving assignment.

Teach a lesson on solving community problems, raising questions such as: What are the problems? How do you find out what they are? What needs to be done to solve the problem?

Teach a lesson on predicting. Have students predict and write their own ending to stories.

Teach word-problem solving strategies in math. Teach students how to identify the information, determine what the problem is asking for, and encourage them to look for word clues that will help decide the operation needed to solve the problem.

Conduct a lesson on mazes. Divide the class into cooperative groups. Each group will design a maze and guide a blindfolded member of the class through the maze using words only.

Provide a variety of puzzles for students to solve. Vary the activity by distributing puzzle shapes to different students. Student will then work together to assemble complete puzzles.

Jane Boyd

Teach a lesson on questioning, stressing key words used in questions and the kinds of answers elicited with the specific key words.

FIGURE A.14
A design for a thematic unit plan on "Mysteries" (intermediate or above)

···· INDEX ····

Activities, culminating, 14
Acts of Meaning, 5
Adolescence, and research-oriented thematic units, 14, 83
Affective domain, 57
Agriculture, committee sub-topic example, 91
Analysis level, Bloom's Taxonomy, 37
Ancess, J., 40
Andre, T., 25
Anecdotal records, 39, 68
Anthropology, 59
Application level, Bloom's Taxonomy, 36
Arends, R., 15
Armstrong, T., 20, 53
Assessment. *See also* Behavioral objectives; Evaluation;
    Portfolio assessment; Test items
  anecdotal records, 39, 68
  authentic, 16, 39–40, 96
  journals, 16, 22, 39, 65, 68, 92, 96
  photographs, 39, 68, 96
  pupil-teacher conferences, 39, 68, 96
Art
  artifacts, 56
  constructions and projects, 3, 7, 16, 22, 26, 33, 56, 59, 68,
    96
  media, 13
  research questions, 91
Ashton-Warner, S., 116
Attitude surveys, 39
Attitudinal objectives, 35
Audio recordings, 39, 59, 92
Audio-visual equipment and materials, 16, 28
Authentic assessment. *See* Assessment; Portfolio
    assessment
Azwell, T., 83

Barker, L. L., 38
Barr, R., 21
Barth, R. S., 116
Behavior, management. *See* Classroom management
Behavioral objectives. *See also* Research-oriented thematic
    unit planning; Thematic unit planning
  and creativity in teaching, 55
  limitations, 38, 68, 96
  writing criteria, 35–36
Bergmann, V. E., 5
Berk, L. E., 13
Bloom, Benjamin, 36
Bloom's Taxonomy, 36–37
Bodily-kinesthetic intelligence, 5, 15
Bondi, J., 118
Borich, G. D., 40
Brainstorming, in unit planning, 58–59, 89–92
  checklist, 59
  research-oriented thematic units, 87, 89–92
  thematic units, 55, 58–59
Brainstorming webs. *See* Web designs
Brandt, R., 5
Brave New Schools, 27
Bright, G. W.,
Brooks, J. G., 20
Brooks, M. G., 20
Bruner, J., 5, 12, 33
Burke, J. B., 21

Cangelosi, J. S., 41
Carey, L., 36
Carlitz, R. D., 119
*Carnegie Council's Task Force on Education of Young
    Adolescents*, 5

Carr, J. F., 26
Case, R., 5, 12
CD-ROM, 16, 27
Cegala, D. J., 36
Centration, centered thinking, 4, 12
Change process, educational, 116–120
   factors, 118
   Oliva model, 118
   six-phases, 118
   staff considerations, 119
   support needs, 118–119
   teacher reluctance, 116–117
Channon, G., 116
Charbonneau, M. P. 33, 40, 59, 89
Charles, C. M., 21
Charts, 7, 59
Chatterton, Roland, 117
Checklists
   brainstorming, 59
   learning center, 47
Cheesebrough, D., 48
Child development, and interdisciplinary instruction,
      12–17
   adolescence, 14, 83
   early childhood, 6, 12–14, 56–57
   middle childhood, 14–17
Claris Works, 27
Classroom exchanges, via internet 27
Classroom management, 21–24
Clay, 56
Closure, 41, 42, 65
Cognitive development
   influences, 13
   levels of objectives and questions, 36–37
   and thematic studies, 4
Cognitive styles. *See* Learning styles; Working styles
Committees, student. *See also* Research-oriented thematic
      unit planning
   forming, 95
   reporting methods, 16
   in research-oriented thematic studies, 15, 83, 85, 89
Completion test items, 41–42
Comprehension level, Bloom's Taxonomy, 36
Computer(s)
   and interdisciplinary instruction, 27, 119
   networking, 16, 33, 119
   software, 7,16, 33, 54, 59, 86, 97
   technology, 14, 59
Concept development, 3, 4, 5–6
Concepts, and the spiraling curriculum, 33
Concrete experiences, 14, 56, 68, 78
Concrete operational thought, 14
Conferences, pupil-teacher, 39, 96
Constructions. *See* Art

Constructivism, constructivist approach, 62
Consultants
   guest speakers, 69
   special area teachers, 97, 117
Consumerism, 59
Content objectives, 35
Convergent questions, 37–38
Cooperative learning, 13, 59, 83. *See also* Committees
Cooperative Learning in the Classroom, 83
Core curriculum, 5
Craver, S., 21
Creative activities. *See* Art; Dance; Drama
Cross Subject Teaching, 117
Culminating activities, 14, 93, 95
Cummins, J., 27
Current events, 59
Curriculum
   change, 116–120
   integrated, 117
   middle school, 111
   guides, 2, 56, 86, 123
   traditional, 4

Dance, 7, 16
Darling-Hammond, L., 40
Davies, I. K., 36
Davis, G. A., 41
Dembo, M., 15, 36
Demonstrations, 16, 57, 59
Dennison, G., 116
Departmentalization
   effect on interdisciplinary instruction, 26
   unit planning modifications, 111–114
Descriptions
   lesson and activity, 65
   research process, 85, 92–95, 106–110
Deserts of the United States, research-oriented thematic
      unit plan example, 97–111
Dewey, J., 3
Diagram, unit plan, 53, 85. *See also* Web designs
Dick, W., 36
Digital cameras, 28
Dioramas, 56
Directions poster, learning center, 48
Discipline, professional approach, 22
Disciplines, academic, 3, 5, 6
Displays, 16
Divergent questions, 37–38
Domains, 2, 3, 6, 16, 57
Drama, 7, 59, 109
Dreeben, R., 21
Duck, L., 21
Dunn, K., 25
Dunn, R., 25

E-mail, 27–28, 91–92

Early childhood development, and thematic unit design, 12–14, 56–57

Ecology, 59, 90

Economics, 59, 90

Education of All Handicapped Children Act, Public Law 94-142, 7

Educational change. *See* Change

Educational philosophy, 21

Educational television, 28

Eggan, P., 15, 53

Egocentrism and egocentricity, 12–13, 56

Eight-step process, interdisciplinary unit design. *See* Research-oriented thematic unit planning; Thematic unit planning

Ellis, A. K., 24, 38, 40, 86

Engel, B. S., 40

Envisioning, lesson planning concept, 64

Essay test items, 42–43

Evaluation. *See also* Assessment; Behavioral objectives; Portfolio assessment; Test items
  and interdisciplinary instruction, 38–45, 68
  methods, 38
  research-oriented thematic unit, 16
  thematic unit, 54, 56

Evaluation level, Bloom's Taxonomy, 37

Examinations. *See* Testing

Experience background, 55, 57

Experimentalist philosophy, 21

Experiments, 33, 56, 59, 96

Falk, B., 40

Family living, 59

Feldman, D. H., 38

Field trip(s), planning, 16, 55, 57, 59–66

Fill-in (completion) test items, 41–42

Films, 16, 28, 33, 54, 59, 86, 97, 120

Filmstrip projectors, 28

Filmstrips, 16, 33, 54, 59, 86, 120

Fisk, L., 48

Fizzell, R., 25

Flavell, J. 12–13

Formal operational thought, 14

Forman, E. A., 6, 12

Foyle, H., 83

Fredericks, A., 48

Frymier, J. R., 118

Funding for interdisciplinary instruction, 119

Furth, H., 13

Future, concept of, 59–60

Gardner, H., 3–5, 12–13, 15, 20, 25, 38

General objectives, 34–35, 53, 67, 84, 95–96
  examples, 35, 70–71, 98

lesson plan, 54, 55, 84
  unit plan, 55, 56, 84, 85

Genocide, 8

Geography, 59, 90

Global studies, 59

Good Apple, 28

Graphic web. *See* Web designs

Graphs, 7, 59, 61, 92, 96

Gronlund, N. E., 36

Gross, B., 116

Gross, R., 116

Grosvenor, L. 40

Group activities. *See* Committees; Cooperative learning

Guest speakers. *See* Consultants

Hands-on learning. *See* Concrete experiences

Health, 59, 91

Henriquez, Milagros, 8

Hentoff, N., 116

Hertz-Lazarowitz, R., 15

History, 8, 13, 59–60

Holocaust, 8

Holt, J., 116

Holubec, E. J., 83

Human behavior, 59

Human relations, 59, 60

Human rights, 8

Humphreys, A., 86

Hypothetical thinking, 14

In Search of Understanding: The Case for Constructivist Classrooms, 27

Information processing, 14

Inhelder, B., 4

Inquiry, 3

Instructional concerns, 24–28
  informational sources, 8
  learning principles, 24–25
  learning styles, 25
  levels, 36
  team teaching, 25–27
  technology, 27–28
  thinking and reasoning, 56
  unit planning, 24

Interdisciplinary method
  benefits, 120–121
  characteristics, 2–3
  flexibility, 7
  rationale, 4–8, 120–121
  reporting methods, 7–8
  teaching skills, 121

Interdisciplinary theme(s), selecting, 32–33, 87
  research-oriented thematic units, 2, 3, 87
  thematic units, 2

Interdisciplinary theme(s) *(continued)*
  widening horizons approach, 32
  spiraling curriculum approach, 33
Interdisciplinary units. *See also* Research-oriented thematic
    unit planning; Thematic unit planning
  central theme, 2
  and child development, 12–17
  distinguishing features, 2–3
  process and content, 3
Interest. *See* Motivation and motivational factors
Intermediate grades, 14. *See also* Departmentalized
    intermediate and middle schools
International Education and Resource Network, 27
Internet
  networking, 27
  skills, 14
  teaching resources, 28
  unit activities, 59, 104, 111
Interpersonal intelligence, 5, 61
Interviews, research
  and linguistic intelligence, 5
  and special needs students, 7, 88
  in thematic units, 59
Intrapersonal intelligence, 5
Introduction, unit plan, 56

Jacobs, H., 3, 24, 59, 89
Johnson, D. W., 83
Johnson, D. T., 83
Johnston, P., 38
Johnston, P. H., 22, 39
Jones, V., 21
Jones, L., 21
Joplin plan, 26
Journal(s), journal entries
  attitudes and feelings, 22, 92
  interdisciplinary unit(s), 68, 76, 92
  in portfolios, 16, 39, 68, 92
  teachers', 68, 96

Kagan, D., 25
Kagan, S., 15
Kamii, C., 24
Kaplan, S. N., 48
Kauchak, D., 15, 53
Kellough, N. G., 87
Kellough, R. D., 87, 89, 53
Key School, 14–15
Kibler, R. J., 36
Kids Network, 27
Kiefer, B. Z., 3, 22, 40, 58, 89
Kimpston, R., 21
Knowledge level, Bloom's Taxonomy, 36
Kohl, H., 116
Kourilsky, M., 41

Kozol, J., 116

Language arts. *See also* Reading; Listening; Speaking;
    Writing
  in interdisciplinary units, 59, 109
  learning center activities, 67
  literature, 2, 8
LCD projectors, 28
Learning center, 45–48, 66–67
  advantages, 45
  checklist, 47
  directions poster, 48
  example, 66–67
  planning, 45–48
  task card, 46
  types, 45–46
Learning preferences, 16. *See also* Multiple intelligences;
    Learning styles; Working styles
Learning principles, 24–25, 62
Learning styles, 13, 25, 59, 62, 85, 87, 91. *See also* Multiple
    intelligences: Working styles
Learning Styles and the Brain, 25
Lecturing. *See* Verbal instruction
Lentz, M., 119
Leonard, G. B., 117
Lescher, M. L., 40
Lesson and unit length, estimating, 53, 54, 83
Lesson planning. *See also* Research-oriented unit planning;
    Thematic unit planning
  closure, 65
  initial, introductory, 53, 55, 92–93
  and multiple intelligences, 53
  new style lesson plan, 53
  procedural elements, 64
  student responses, 64
Letter writing, 7, 91
Levstik, L. S., 3, 22, 40, 58, 89
Lindemann, R. H., 41
Lindgren, H., 48
Linguistic intelligence, 5, 61
Listening, 57, 59, 67, 76, 109
Literature, children's, 2, 8
Logical-mathematical intelligence, 5, 61
Lyman, L., 83

McNeil, J. D., 53
Magazines, 33, 86, 119
Mager, R., 36
Management, behavior. *See* Classroom management
Maps, 7, 16, 93
Matching test items, 44–45
Materials
  effect on planning, 33
  instructional, 14, 54, 69, 120
  sources, 8

Mathematics, 67, 93
  in interdisciplinary studies, 3, 7, 56, 61, 67
  as isolated subject, 27
  learning center activities, 67
  and logical-mathematical intelligence, 5, 61
  talented students, 14
  and testing, 38, 40
Media, 33
Merenda, P. F., 41
MI curriculum, 14
Middle childhood, development, 14–17
Middle schools, 14. *See also* Departmentalized
      intermediate and middle schools
Miles, D. T., 38
Miller, E., 116, 119
Mills, Joyce Schonberger, 117
Minick, N., 6, 12
Motivation and motivational factors
  behavior, 21
  child development, 88
  committee work, 83
  evaluation, 38, 69
  individual interests, 13, 16, 91
  interest surveys, 39
  learning principle, 62
  learning styles, 25
  participation, 22, 86
  team teaching, 26
  theme selection, 2, 33, 87
  unit development, 34, 62–63, 93–94
Movement activities, 13, 61. *See also* Dance
Multicultural education, 8, 59, 60, 87, 116
Multidisciplinary instruction, 117. *See also*
      Interdisciplinary instruction
Multimedia, 27, 59
Multiple-choice test items, 44
Multiple Intelligences in the Classroom, 20
Multiple intelligences
  instructional implications, 5, 13, 20, 55, 85
  MI curriculum, 14
  MI lesson plan, 53
  theory, 4–5, 20
Murals, 59, 60, 61, 92
Music, 13, 16, 57, 61
Musical intelligence, 5, 14

National Council for the Social Studies (NCSS), 86
National Education Association, 83
National Geographic Society, 27
NCSS Task Force, 14
Neo-Piagetian research. *See* Post-Piagetian research
Networking, 14, 16, 27, 33, 119
New York City Teacher Centers Consortium, 28
New York Learning Link, 27
New York Times Educational Media, 28

Newspapers, 33, 77, 86
Notes. *See also* Notetaking skills
  journal, 68
  on learning materials, 86
  pupil-teacher conference, 68
  student portfolio, 39
  teachers', 68, 97
Notetaking skills, 5, 16, 27, 88, 96

Objectives, 34-36. *See also* Behavioral objectives; General
      objectives
  affective and attitudinal, 35, 67, 71, 84, 98
  cognitive, content, and concept, 67, 70–71, 84, 85, 98
  process, 35, 67, 71, 84
  specific, 34
  unit planning, 34–35
Observational skills, 39, 60
Observation(s)
  student, 39, 61, 68
  teacher, 39, 68, 96
Ogan, B. J., 83
Oliva, P. F., 118
Online services, 14, 16, 27
Operational knowledge, 6
Oral presentations, 7, 16, 28, 82
Oregon Trail, 27
O'Neil, H. F., 25
O'Neil, J., 40
Osborn, D. K., 21
Osborn, J., 21
Overhead projectors, 28
Ozman, H. L., 21

Painting, sand, 91
Panel discussions, 16
Pappas, C. C., 3, 22, 40, 58, 89
Performing arts, 59. *See also* Dance; Music
Phye, G. D., 25
Phillips, J., 12
Philosophy, and the interdisciplinary teacher, 21
Photographs, 39, 68, 96
Piaget, J.
  adaptation theory, 24
  influence on instruction, 5–6, 12
  and post-Piagetian research, 56
  and Vygotsky, 5–6, 12
Pines, M., 116
Planning, student involvement, 13, 26
Planning strategies, general, 34–48. *See also* Assessment;
      Behavioral objectives; Learning centers; Test items
  evaluation methods, 38–45
  instructional levels, 36–37
  questioning, 37–38
  objective(s), preparing, 34–36
Play dough, 56

Political science, 59

Poppe, C. A., 48

Portfolio assessment
  in interdisciplinary units, 16, 54
  materials, 16, 39–40, 65, 86, 96
  strengths and limitations, 40

Post, R., 86

Post-Piagetian research
  differences with Piaget, 14, 56
  support for interdisciplinary instruction, 12

Postman, N., 116

Preoperational thought, 12, 56, 57

Principles of learning, 24–25, 62

Problem-solving, 5, 6, 15, 27, 36, 46, 59, 67, 75

Procedure, in lesson plans, 54

Process vs. content, 3

Process objectives, 35

Projects. See also Art
  individual and group, 83, 86, 92
  interdisciplinary unit, 7, 39, 93

Proximity, and modifying student behavior, 23

Psychology, 59, 60

Psychomotor domain, 57

Public Law 94-142, The Education of All Handicapped
      Children Act, 7

Pupil-teacher conferences, 39, 68, 96

Puppet shows, 16, 92

Purposes, general, 55

Putnam, J. G., 21

Quaranta, L., 41

Questions
  convergent and divergent, 37–38
  for guiding student research, 85, 90

Rain Forest, 27

Ravich, D., 32

Readability, and test validity, 40

Reading
  activities in interdisciplinary studies, 3, 14
  independent level, 14, 57, 87, 88
  intermediate grade and middle school students, 12, 14,
      83
  as isolated subject, 26
  and logical-mathematical intelligence, 5
  and learning centers, 46
  and notetaking, 88
  oral, 39, 57
  and research, 54
  student difficulties, 7, 13
  and test reliability, 40, 68
  and unit planning, 33

Reading teacher, 111, 113

Reconstructionist philosophy, 21

Recordings, audio and video, 39, 54

Reed, J. S., 5

Reider, B. E. 33, 40, 59, 89

Reliability test, 40-41

Reporting, alternative methods, 7–8, 91

Reports, student, 16, 59

Requirements of interdisciplinary teachers, 20–24

Research
  on interdisciplinary methodology, 118
  phases, 92–93
  process, 82
  and special needs children, 7
  strategies, 59

Research-oriented thematic unit planning, 81–114
  brainstorming procedure, 58, 87–89
  and child development, 87, 88
  committees, 15–16, 82, 83, 90
  and departmentalized schools, 111–113
  distinguishing features, 15, 54, 82–83
  eight-step planning process, 87
  evaluating, 16–17, 86, 87, 96–97
  field trips, 16
  materials, 85, 86, 87, 97
  objectives, 84, 85, 94, 95–96
  oral presentations, 82
  overview, 15–17
  outline, 83–86
  planning phase, 15, 86, 92–95
  reporting phase, 16, 82, 86, 93, 94–95
  research phase, 86, 93, 95
  sample unit plan, 98–111
  theme selection, 2, 3, 87
  titles, 87, 97
  topics, 83

Reversibility, reversals in early childhood, 13

Richardson, Elwyn, 3, 116

Roberts, P. L., 53, 89

Rottier, J., 83

Sand painting, 92

Santrock, J. W., 13–14

Sayers, D., 27

Scannell, D. P., 41

Schmuck, R., 15

Science
  activities in interdisciplinary studies, 3, 7, 55, 56
  committees in research-oriented thematic units,
      90
  equipment and materials, 8, 33, 47, 97, 120
  and intermediate grade and middle school students,
      25, 111, 113
  in learning centers, 46, 67
  and student portfolios, 68
  student research questions, 90, 101
  and unit themes, 2, 32

Scientific method, 7, 71

Seventh Grade Slump, The, 5
Sharan, S., 15
Short answer test items, 41
Silberman, C. E., 116
Skills
  inquiry, 7
  and interdisciplinary instruction, 3, 6–7
  lessons, 59, 87–88, 91
  locational, 16
  notetaking, 5, 16, 27
  observational, 60
Skits, 16
Slavery, 8
Slavin, R., 15
Slide shows, 28
Social interaction, 5–6, 12
Social studies
  activities in interdisciplinary studies, 56, 61, 76
  equipment and materials, 8, 93, 97, 119–120
  intermediate grade and middle school students, 86
  traditional approach, 4
  unit themes, 2, 32–33, 86
Sociology, 59, 60
Software concerns, computer
  supply, 33, 86
  materials for students, 7, 16, 27, 54, 69, 97
  materials for teachers, 27, 28
  special needs students, 88
Space exploration, 59
Spaces and Places, 3
Spatial intelligence, 5, 61
Speaking, 59
Special area teachers, 25, 117
Special needs students
  and activity alternatives, 14, 88
  benefits of interdisciplinary method, 7, 120
Specific objectives, 35. *See also* Behavioral objectives
Spiraling curriculum, 33
Spring, thematic unit plan example, 70–78
Stephens, L. S., 58
Stevenson, C., 26
Stockton, W., 21
Stone, C. A., 6, 12
Student involvement and participation
  determining unit titles, 97
  investing concept, 13, 22, 26, 62, 69, 82, 87
  and unit planning, 13, 14
Subject-centered approach, 4, 5
Substance abuse, 59
Sunburst Communications, 28
Surveys, 39, 59
Synthesis level, Bloom's Taxonomy, 37

Talents, 14, 57, 88, 102
Task card, 46, 67

Teacher
  networks, 119
  observations, 39
  responsibilities, 16
Teaching requirements for interdisciplinary instruction, 20–24
Team teaching
  in departmentalized schools, 113
  and interdisciplinary instruction, 25–26
Technology, 27–28. *See also* Computers
Telecommunications. *See* Computers; Technology
Television, 32
  educational, 28, 69
Testing and test items, 40–45
  completion (fill-in), 41–42
  essay, 42–43
  limitations, 38
  matching, 44–45
  multiple-choice, 44
  short answer, 41
  true/false, 43
  unit, 77, 96, 110
Tests. *See* Testing and test items
Textbooks
  alternatives, 20, 60
  methods, 33, 41
  need for variety, 8, 97, 110, 119, 120
  and oral reading, 57
  and reporting, 7
  and research-oriented unit planning, 86, 93
  and test construction, 42
  and thematic unit planning, 47, 54
  themes and topics, 32
Thematic studies, description, 3
Thematic unit planning, 51–79
  brainstorming procedure, 55, 58–61
  and child development, 12–14, 56–57
  design, 33–34
  distinguishing features, 12–14
  eight-step planning process, 55–56
  evaluating, 68
  field trips, 55, 57, 59, 60, 61, 63–65, 66
  initial, introductory lesson plan, 52, 53, 62–65
  initial unit plan, 55
  length, 60
  lesson and activity descriptions, 65–67
  materials, 69
  objectives, 52, 53, 54, 56, 65, 67
  outline, 52–54
  sample unit plan, 70–78
  student involvement, 13
  theme selection, 2
  titles, 69–70
  web, 58–62
Theme research projects, 6

Themes, interdisciplinary
  central, 3, 82
  environmental, 86
  traditional and non-conventional, 2
  selecting, 12–13, 32, 56–57, 87
Thinking and reasoning skills, 3, 12, 56
Time, concept, 13
Time lines, 59, 60
Timeliner, 27, 92, 104
Titles, unit plan, 52, 53, 56, 69–70, 83, 97
Tom Snyder Productions, 27
Topic selection, widening horizons approach, 33, 83
Tracy, D. B., 41
Trade books, 8, 54, 119
Traditional approach, 4
Transformational thought, 13
True/false test items, 43

Unit and lesson length, estimating, 53, 54, 83
Unit plan design, 33, 55. *See also* Research-oriented
      thematic unit planning; Thematic unit
      planning
United Federation of Teachers, 28

Valentine, M. R., 21
Validity, in testing, 40
Values clarification, 59
Van Matre, N. A. 48
Vars, G. F., 26
Verbal instruction, 6, 57
Verbal intelligence, 5
Viadero, D., 25, 40
Video programs and presentations, 16, 33, 59, 97,
      119
Video recordings, 39
Visual arts, 59. *See also* Art constructions and
      projects

Vygotsky, L. S.
  and Piaget, 5–6, 12
  theory, 6, 12
  zone of proximal development (ZPD), 6

Wadsworth, B., 13
Wakefield, A. P., 7
Wasserstein, P. 40
Ways of knowing, 3, 6, 55, 83, 120
Web designs, brainstorming
  alternative approaches, 58, 89, 123–137
  concept and idea webs, 58, 64
  in departmentalized programs, 112
  research-oriented unit planning, 89, 99, 112
  thematic unit planning, 58, 60–62, 72
Webb, C., 15
Weingartner, C., 116
Wertsch, J. V., 6, 12
Wexler-Sherman, C., 38
WNET, 28
Widening horizons approach, 32–33
Wiles, J., 53, 118
Williamson, R., 26
Woolfolk, A. E., 41
Workbooks, 5
Working styles, 55, 59, 65, 82, 83, 91, 96. *See also*
      Learning styles; Multiple intelligences
Writing
  activities, 3, 7, 67
  and interdisciplinary studies, 39, 83
  in learning centers, 67
  and linguistic intelligence, 5
  and portfolio assessment, 68, 96
  reports, 91
  skills, 3, 33, 83

Zone of proximal development (ZPD), 6